Policing

Is About **People**

Policing

Is About **People**

Special Agent (Retired)
Martin J. Schwartz

DIANE,
THANK YOU FOR YOUR SERVICE!
BEST WISHES!

SA(RET) #136
(2019)

ARCHWAY
PUBLISHING

This book is a work of non-fiction. Unless otherwise noted, the author and the publisher make no explicit guarantees as to the accuracy of the information contained in this book and in some cases, names of people and places have been altered to protect their privacy.

Archway Publishing books may be ordered through booksellers or by contacting:

Archway Publishing
1663 Liberty Drive
Bloomington, IN 47403
www.archwaypublishing.com
1 (888) 242-5904

Because of the dynamic nature of the Internet, any web addresses or links contained in this book may have changed since publication and may no longer be valid. The views expressed in this work are solely those of the author and do not necessarily reflect the views of the publisher, and the publisher hereby disclaims any responsibility for them.

Any people depicted in stock imagery provided by Getty Images are models, and such images are being used for illustrative purposes only. Certain stock imagery © Getty Images.

ISBN: 978-1-4808-8105-1 (sc)
ISBN: 978-1-4808-8106-8 (hc)
ISBN: 978-1-4808-8104-4 (e)

Library of Congress Control Number: 2019912272

Print information available on the last page.

Archway Publishing rev. date: 8/28/2019

About the Cover

The cover of this book is a painting that hangs proudly in my home. I am sincerely grateful to the artist, retired Philadelphia firefighter Richard Popolow, for allowing me to use it as the cover for this book.[1] The painting was given to me by my staff toward the end of my career when I commanded an insurance fraud unit. The names on the lockers were close friends, most of whom have gone end of watch.

Bill Wright died much too young of what we would call natural causes, but I am convinced he was a victim of the job.

Rick O'Brien was my partner for many years. Somehow, we both survived policing.

Michael O'Donnell was one of the best officers I ever knew. I worked for Mike several times during my career. One of my great honors was serving on his funeral detail.

Ippolito Gonzalez was a superhuman whom I had the privilege of knowing and working with. Lee was murdered on a car stop. I had the honor of serving on his funeral detail along with other fine officers.

Acknowledgments

I cannot remember everyone who enabled me to serve more than forty years in law enforcement. Some I worked with and for. Some were mentors, and some were role models—whether they knew it or not. Some are cops, and many are not, but they all made me better. To name just a few would insult the many, too numerous to recall. I am grateful for every one of them.

To those of you who were more than all of that,
you know who you are and what you did.
To you, especially, I am forever grateful. I will never forget you.

Chuck, thanks for the friendship, counsel,
and for modeling police resiliency.

To my editor—my wife, Nancy—I could not
have done it without you. Thank you.

For all the people I tried to help—who gave
so much more to me than I returned.
Especially to those of you who are the soul
of America. You know who you are.
This book is for you.

Contents

Preface

"Nobody likes a cop," were the words of wisdom my father gave me the day I graduated from the police academy. I did not think much about it at the time, but over the past forty years, I have come to understand what my father meant. My grandfather was a Philadelphia police officer for forty years, so my father experienced policing firsthand. He lived through the violence directed at my grandfather when he was shot by local thugs while attempting to arrest one of their family members. That officer-involved shooting occurred in early 1900 and is not even a blip in the history of the Philadelphia Police Department. When we take a closer look at why that shooting occurred that day, the reasons echo loudly even today, and the noise will continue for years to come.

My grandfather was a large, tall man with broad shoulders. He was also an athlete and a swift runner who won many city races as a member of the Philadelphia Police Department. One day, local neighborhood ruffians were intoxicated, fighting, and generally causing a ruckus. My grandfather, at the behest of the citizenry, carried out his duties and intervened. A struggle ensued, and he was able to effect an arrest on one of the rowdies. As he moved with the arrestee to a call box to request assistance from the district house, another combatant produced a double-barreled shotgun and peppered him in the back and legs. My grandfather held fast to the suspect, dragged him to a nearby call box, and called for assistance. Officers arrived from the district house at Belgrade and Clearfield Streets and quelled the Port Richmond fray for that day.

Those ruffians shot my grandfather because he was intervening, preventing, and otherwise interfering with the disturbance they were intent on creating. He was doing something that I write about in the following chapters. I dissect the word *reasonableness* as it applies to police interactions with people and as set forth in the Fourth Amendment to the United States Constitution.

My father saw my grandfather become the target of attacks from their neighbors when he was called to strike duty during the labor wars of the day, and his duties became physical and violent. Sometimes those duties required him to arrest his neighbors. As a young boy, my father had trouble understanding how these pleasant neighbors changed from cordial and friendly to mean people uttering unkind words to his father. He too became the target of these attacks as his school chums ridiculed him merely because his father was a cop. Where did those children—his soccer pals and classmates—learn this hatred?

My father also watched his father become the savior of the neighborhood when locals knocked on his front door at all hours of the day and night because they needed help from a cop. A wife assaulted by her drunken husband, parents with an unruly adolescent, a family member arrested, a lost child—they all knocked on my grandfather's door because they needed a cop.

Many years later, my grandfather, who was an old man by then, was sitting on his stoop when a local thug came along, mugged him, and stole his wallet. I think the mugging bothered him more than being shot. On the day he was shot, he was doing his duty. He was a cop. On the day he was mugged, he was an old man who was attacked by a predator preying on the old and weak. He knew what that was. He spent a lifetime fighting it.

There is no fairy-tale ending to my grandfather's story. He became quieter, more detached, lonelier, and generally angrier as he aged. Although to me as a young boy, he was my grandpop, I recall the unhappiness on his face that I now understand. My grandfather died of what we call natural causes. However, there is little doubt that his years of policing contributed to his death.

My father did not follow his father to the job. He would go on to a different hell with his career in the military. While stationed in the Panama Canal zone, he saw signs that read, "Soldiers and Dogs Keep Off the Grass." He experienced combat and years of violence in both World War II and Korea. He was shot on the island of Luzon in the Philippines when General Douglas MacArthur returned. In his old age, my father became a man very similar to my grandfather.

I decided to write this book while I was on a hunting trip in Pennsylvania. I did not get anything on the trip other than cold and wet, but it was an excellent opportunity to hang out with a few cops who worked for me earlier in their careers. These are members of my blue family. I am proud of their career progression, and being with them inspired me to focus, more than usual, on the last forty years of my career. After all these years, cops are still my family. I am more comfortable with another cop than I am with pretty much anyone else. I love cops, but I don't always like them.

I served more than forty years in law enforcement at federal, state, and local levels and in the military. I served in the United States Air Force as a security policeman before the name changed to what may be the more appropriate name "security forces" that we know now. I was a municipal police officer, a state criminal investigator, and a United States special agent.

The chapters in this book are not made up of war stories about my career. Nobody wants to read about them, and I have no desire to tell them. I do have a desire—in fact, I believe a responsibility—to talk about policing. Throughout my career, I have held to one constant, and it is that policing is about people. If I were to try to define policing, the one word I would have to include, without hesitation, is the word *people*.

In this book, I write about the militarization of the police, which is a topic frequently discussed by police critics. I write about how the use of military equipment and tactics have impacted police operations and the public perceptions that exist as a result.

I write about the health and well-being of police officers and how they may impact our daily interactions with people. How does what cops see, hear, and feel affect them, and how resilient are they to those affects? I write about violent use-of-force encounters and fear, and I examine policing from many facets because policing is multifaceted.

The purpose of government—and as an extension of the government, law enforcement—is to take care of its people. The government provides structure, resources, and services for its people. Policing mottos across this country are some variation of "To protect and serve." Police are protecting and serving the people of our communities. Every action I took in my law enforcement career had, at its core, a focus on people. Sometimes the nexus between policing and people is difficult to see. When that happens, policing becomes confusing and hard for the public to understand.

Policing is about people, and when policing is effective, the police and the people are in harmony. When cops go home at the end of a shift, they take the job home. They are always a cop and always a part of the community they police. Cops who patrol violent high-crime areas take the aura of those neighborhoods home with them. It is not something they leave behind. There may be time clocks in police departments, but they are there for the bean counters. The cop does not punch out. Cops take everything with them, at home and in recreation. It never leaves them.

This book is about the policing profession that I love. A profession that, unfortunately and to my detriment, has meant more to me than anything else in my life. Mental health professionals have plenty of diagnoses for it, but there it is. The theme throughout each chapter of this book is *policing is about people*. The theme does not change when I write about policing an inner city, a suburban town, or rural America. The police are the people, and the people are the police.

I write candidly about the police with no attempt to justify or cover up that we can sometimes be wrong. I do not back down from things we do right, even when they are not popular. The police have a hard job, but all people have hard jobs. Life is not easy for most of us. If life were easy, the entertainment industry would not be the big escape from reality that it is for so many.

I write about the law of the land that determines the appropriateness of police actions, and I examine causes of real, positive changes we are seeing in police officers. The chapters of this book will explore the differences between us but more importantly the similarities that bind us as a people. The "black lives matter" and "blue lives matter" movements may not be as opposite as they appear, and the "all lives matter" believers may be missing the point.

Every time a cop dies, I experience myriad emotions. Cops who needlessly die because they were driving too fast, not wearing a seat belt, or engaging in other such behavior both saddens and angers me because it was unnecessary. I am saddened and proud of every cop who is assaulted and killed in the line of duty. I understand that our officers are in harm's way every single day. It is part of the job. I am both sad and angry at every cop who dies by his or her own hand. I am angry at that cop for choosing suicide as the solution, angry at that cop for the people he or she left behind, and sad that we lost an officer.

Moreover, I am angry at the unprovoked assassinations of our officers that we see all too often lately. My anger over Sergeant Ippolito Gonzalez's murder is not of the initial shooting. I accept that our cops are in harm's way. My anger comes from deep inside of me because his assassination occurred after he was incapacitated. There is a special kind of evil in a person who does that.

I have experienced countless emotions throughout my career. I have been angry at the injustices of the criminal justice system that does not always get it right. The hopelessness and despair I saw in homes saddened me because only police officers experience what occurs in the privacy of a family's home during the worst of times. I am saddened every time I see a young person shot and killed by the police.

The environmental injustices I saw in both rural America and our inner cities sadden me. I am saddened by the poverty of malnourished children without beds to sleep in or toys to play with who do not even know how to play. I am saddened seeing people unable to heat their houses and be warm in winter. I am also sad for other officers who see similar scenarios. There is nothing that can prepare a person for what an officer sees, and when the officer thinks she has pretty much seen it all, something happens that is worse. These images, scenes, and memories will be with her forever.

There is the memory of two little girls seated at a card table in an unfurnished, cold home. They are wearing coats because there is little or no heat in the house. There is a cupcake on the table because it is one of the little girls' birthdays. She has nothing. The family has nothing, and there is little chance they ever will. It will take a miracle. The cops do not have time to stay. The guy we are looking for is not there, and we have another call.

There is a little girl terrified by the domestic trauma she witnessed. No one should see what she saw. No one should ever be that terrified, especially a little child. The next day, she is riding her tricycle down the sidewalk and waves to the police car on patrol because the sight of that cop reminds her of the only sane thing that happened in her young life.

These memories are of people. Sometimes bad memories fade. Sometimes bad memories become distant and are replaced by pleasant ones. To police officers though, the memories never leave. They may not think of them every day, but they do not leave. They become a part of who we are. We never forget the people.

In this age of territorial flag planting, I should clearly state at the outset that I think I am a conservative. If that does not sound very certain, it is getting less so all of the time. I say that because I watch little Fox News, and I mostly watch CNN. I do not watch Fox often because I want to hear other points of view instead of ones I already understand. I watch CNN because I want to hear other points of view, which can be contrary to mine. I want to hear, and I listen carefully.

I am not an environmentalist, but you will read about my compassion for people who have been victimized by abuses to the environment. You will read about the people of a community who became collateral damage in America's quest for energy. At the same time, you will read my acknowledgment of the importance of energy independence, my understanding that we still need fossil fuels, and my knowledge that fracking is not going away.

You will read about my love for cops, my defense of cops, my forgiveness for cops who do not get it right, and my never-ending quest to make them better and keep them safe. You will also read about my openness to the concerns of people who look, think, and feel differently than I do. You will read about my attempts not just to listen but to understand an opposing point of view and, where possible, find a commonness in our beliefs.

The commonness of the United States Constitution that guarantees certain protections for all people is a good starting point. We, the police who are the people, and we, the people who are the police. We must agree to zealously guard the protections of the people as guaranteed in our Constitution and, more specifically, in the Fourth Amendment. A failure to do so will continue to spiral us toward mistrust, hatred, and violence and will result in needless deaths.

When the police use force, especially deadly force, it is almost always viewed by the public as an infringement of a civil right—the right to be free from unreasonable seizures. What is rarely ever discussed are legitimate officer safety issues, which were the impetus for a change in our teaching methodology. You will read about those changes in subsequent chapters.

Consider the shooting of an unarmed person, the shooting of a person in the back, and the shooting of an unarmed black or brown person in the back. These are about the deprivation of civil rights and not about the use of force. However, the public's observations of police use of force are not always clearly understood, and the force may sometimes seem excessive. The police see the use of force as objectively reasonable. A grand jury or court looks at the incident and further infuriates the public when it determines that the officer's actions were reasonable based upon the Fourth Amendment. How could it be reasonable for the police to shoot an unarmed person? The answer is difficult to understand. The answer is: "It depends."

The fact is that most of the force used by the police in the United States is lawful and reasonable. Many people do not believe that, and the mistrust runs deep. Whenever an incident occurs where the force is perceived to be excessive, the mistrust worsens. I write about cynicism and bias in this book, but suffice to say, we cannot judge police use of force based upon how we feel or what we think. We must judge the reasonableness of all police use of force based on the facts that confronted the officer at the time the force was applied. I see uses of force by the police that I do not like, but I do not base my judgment on whether I like the action. I base my judgment on reasonableness. Maybe the inequities of the criminal justice system and the perception by some of the unfairness of it continue to make fact-driven judgments hard to believe. The suspicion of police cover-ups contributes to this mistrust regardless of whether it is true or not.

The public often believes that suspected police abuses, especially those involving deadly force, should result in the immediate arrest of the officer and a murder charge. They argue that an arrest and murder charge would be the result if a private citizen shot and killed someone. The analogy is flawed, however, because only the facts determine the validity of an arrest. An arrest is only appropriate when the facts reveal that there is probable cause to believe that a crime was committed. That is true whether the shooting occurs by a private citizen or a police officer. Facts drive the result, and police officers are arrested, charged, and convicted when the facts support the process. However, officer-involved shootings generally do not begin with the officer committing a predicate offense such as robbery. That is very different from the scenario of a person, who during the commission of a crime, commits an act of homicide. In that case, the crime is already occurring when the homicide is committed.

The title of this book is the theme of this book. It is about the police, but it is also about people because the police are people, or at least that is what we want them to be. There will be people who will not like or agree with some of the things I wrote here, and that includes cops. However, the deaths we see on our streets are long past likes and dislikes. We must find better ways to solve the differences between us instead of killing each other. We have too many people needlessly dying in our streets.

I want you to read this book if you are a person. Whether you are a police officer or not is not relevant because this is a book about people. It is not a book for cops about cops. It is a book about people, and some of them happen to be cops. A lot are not. If the book does nothing else, I hope it causes you to pause and think about what we all can do to help make interactions between police and people better.

CHAPTER ONE
THE FOURTH AMENDMENT

We do not like to see people shot or officers involved in shootings, but sometimes it happens because it is necessary. Subsequent evaluations of these uses of force are often shown to be reasonable, even the ones we do not like.

Chapter 1
The Fourth Amendment

The right of the people to be secure in their persons,
houses, papers, and effects, against unreasonable searches
and seizures, shall not be violated, and no warrants shall
issue, but upon probable cause, supported by oath or
affirmation, and particularly describing the place to be
searched, and the persons or things to be seized.
—Constitution of the United States of America,
1789 (rev. 1992), Amendment IV

The fifty-four words of the Fourth Amendment are the most important tools the police will ever have. They are more important than any firearm, more important than Sir Robert Peel's[2] theories on policing, and more important than J. Edgar Hoover's national fingerprint file. The Fourth Amendment is the standard required for nearly all police actions. It must be the starting point of any discussion involving the government's policing of its people.

Policing is the duty to maintain law and order. It exists for the protection, safety, and security of the people from personal and property crimes and from those who would do harm. Simply put, policing is about people.

However, policing is about more than that, and not recognizing this responsibility and jealously guarding these protections can contribute to a deterioration of the police and public equilibrium that needs to exist. This equilibrium or balance between the police and the citizenry ensures that people may freely exercise rightful liberties while being safeguarded under the protection of the police. When put this way, policing takes on a whole new meaning. The fact is that it cannot be put any other way because that is what it is. Policing is about people.

When I entered the Criminal Investigator Training Program (CITP) at the Federal Law Enforcement Training Center (FLETC) in Glynco, Georgia, I was a brand-new special agent with twenty-five years of experience as a state and local police officer. My classmates were interested in learning about traditional policing, but I had no interest in becoming a firearms expert, which I already was, or in excelling on the driving tracks, which I did. My interest focused on those fifty-four words. It quickly became apparent to me that understanding the Fourth Amendment was critical for effective policing. Until then, I knew I was a good cop, but I soon learned that a better understanding of those fifty-four words would make me better.

I have had many mentors during my career, and I remember every one of them. Some I remember for what they taught me to do—and some for what they taught me not to do. The best forced me to think, work out the problem, and ultimately make my best decision.

My Fourth Amendment mentor was a retired United States assistant attorney and the former chairman of the FLETC's legal division. Jim Baker was a hard-nosed former federal prosecutor who had firm opinions about right and wrong. He was a Vietnam veteran and a retired United States Army colonel. With his strong conservative opinion, he was likable to any cop because he thought like we did. To Jim Baker, the law was the law except when it came to the Fourth Amendment. When he interpreted the Fourth Amendment, there was no clear right or wrong answer. To Jim, it depended squarely on the facts. He masterfully digested, analyzed, and filtered the facts through those fifty-four words, and somehow the rights and wrongs would emerge. Jim's initial response to any Fourth Amendment question was "It depends."

Before Jim Baker's tutelage, I started hundreds of search warrant affidavits with the words "This affiant has probable cause to believe." Jim never told me to stop using those words, but I never did again. I realized that my affidavit would be much stronger if I merely stated the facts rather than concluding probable cause. I did not need to give the court the conclusion. I needed to give the judge the facts and allow the probable cause conclusion to become clear.

Throughout my career, I sat in plenty of annual refresher classes where we analyzed police applications of force. These classes focused on what police can and cannot do. More than once the question, "Can you shoot him?" was answered with a simple yes or no. We analyzed reasonableness from the perspective of the actions of the officer. Instead, we should have considered whether the officer's actions were reasonable based upon the rights afforded to the people.

Most of us viewed the word *reasonable* very narrowly. We listened to the facts of a case, usually about an officer-involved shooting, and gave an opinion of whether the officer's actions were reasonable. To reach an answer, we looked at the conclusion, discussed our opinions, and voted by a show of hands. The controversial cases would evoke passionate discussions. Was the shooting justified or not?

That was the way we taught deadly force, and little has changed. Even the most progressive instructors still teach police use of force from the perspective of the reasonableness of the officer and not from the rights of the people. The existing teaching methodology is not wrong, but considering the division in this country, the mistrust of the police, and the felonious assaults on our officers, we can and should be better. To be better, we must shift our way of thinking.

Somewhere over the years, I learned the best way to figure out how to protect something like a person or property is to think about ways to attack it. Only then can one effectively protect it. If we analyze the Fourth Amendment to determine what the police can do, we miss the point. The point is not what the police can do. The point is to understand the rights afforded to the people by the Constitution and ensure we protect those rights. A seizure of a person by the police is then guaranteed by the Constitution to be reasonable.

Essentially, there are two types of laws in the United States: statutes and case law. Statutes are laws enacted by state or federal legislatures and signed into law by a governor or the president. Case law derives from a published court decision made by a judge or a panel of judges who interpret existing statutes and case law and render an opinion.

There are only a few legislated laws, state and federal, that define police conduct. Legislation to enforce laws, carry firearms, and effect arrests are examples. They provide the police with authority to perform their duties. The police develop standard operating procedures based on these responsibilities, and these guide their conduct under normal and emergency operations.

Police agencies are also responsible for complying with directives from lawful authorities, such as a governor, attorney general, local prosecutor, district attorney, or judge. For instance, a local district attorney can tell the police that the prosecutor's office will not prosecute people charged with possession of small quantities of marijuana. This mandate essentially draws police to the conclusion that these arrests are futile and are therefore not made. America, right now, is divided about immigration, which is regulated by federal law. Governors, attorneys general, and even some mayors are instructing the police within their respective authorities not to cooperate with immigration officials in detaining persons wanted only for immigration violations.

Police are also mandated to perform their duties in accordance with case law. A state court can render a decision applicable to its state. A federal district court could render a decision applicable to its district, and the Supreme Court of the United States (the Court) can render a decision applicable to all the United States. *Roe v. Wade,*[3] for example, is the Court decision giving women the right to legal abortions. It has been the law of the land since the Court rendered its decision in 1973.

Consequently, case law significantly affects police conduct and operations. It either reaffirms traditional policing or forces radical change. Two Supreme Court cases that significantly affected police operations are *Miranda v. Arizona*[4] and *Terry v. Ohio.*[5] In *Miranda*, the Court outlined specific rights afforded to people in police custody. *Terry* requires police to be reasonable during investigative stops.

While the decisions in *Miranda* and *Terry* are critically important to policing, *Graham v. Connor*[6] is the leading Supreme Court decision cited by police use-of-force experts. It essentially says that all seizures made by the police must be judged based on the seventeenth word of the Fourth Amendment. They cannot be "unreasonable." A seizure by the police can be as simple as a physical arrest or "collar," a term used by early and mid-twentieth-century police officers, or it can be as severe as a seizure by a bullet fired from a police officer's firearm.

The Court decided *Graham v. Connor* in 1989. Graham, a person with diabetes, had a friend, Berry, take him to a convenience store to purchase orange juice to counteract the onset of an insulin emergency. The men hastily entered and exited the store after seeing too many people waiting in the checkout line. Police officers observing the men determined their actions to be suspicious and consistent with the actions of robbers. They stopped their car to investigate. Unknown to the officers, Graham was suffering from the insulin emergency. When Berry stopped the car, Graham got out, ran around it, and sat down on the curb. His speech was incoherent, and he was not complying with police commands. Graham was handcuffed and sustained injuries due to a physical encounter that ensued. Neither Graham nor his companion violated any laws, and his insulin emergency was determined to be legitimate. At the time police seized Graham, they did not know that the men entered the store to buy orange juice and quickly departed because the store was too busy. Graham filed a federal lawsuit alleging that the police violated his Fourth Amendment protection against an unreasonable seizure.

When rendering its decision in *Graham*, the Court identified several key points relevant to future police conduct. Justice Kennedy, writing the opinion of the Court, said:

> Today we make explicit what was implicit in Garner's (*Tennessee v. Garner*) analysis and hold that all claims that law enforcement officers have used excessive force—deadly or not—in the course of an arrest, investigatory stop, or other "seizure" of a free citizen should be analyzed under the Fourth Amendment and its "reasonableness" standard. The calculus of reasonableness must embody allowance for the fact that police officers are often forced to make split-second judgments—in circumstances that are tense, uncertain, and rapidly evolving— about the amount of force that is necessary in a particular situation. The Fourth Amendment is not capable of precise definition or mechanical application, however, its proper application requires careful attention to the facts and circumstances of each particular case, including the severity of the crime at issue, whether the suspect poses an immediate threat to the safety of the officers or others, and whether he is actively resisting arrest or attempting to evade arrest by flight.[7]

For the first time, the Court established four considerations to be applied when determining the reasonableness of the force used. We must judge the reasonableness of these events from the perspective of the officer on the scene at the time the force was applied and not with the twenty-twenty vision of hindsight. The Court wrote that the severity of the crime, whether the subject poses a risk to the public or other officers, the resistance of a subject to arrest, or attempts to escape by flight should be considerations in evaluating the force used by the police.[8]

The Court decided that these four factors be applied when examining police use of force. They are not an all-inclusive or exhaustive list. Instead, they contribute to the "totality of the circumstances" confronting the officer at the time the officer applied force or seized a person. These factors are critical when determining the reasonableness of police action. As an example, in the absence of other factors, it would not be reasonable for a police officer to seize a shoplifter with a bullet from his firearm. The crime of shoplifting, in and of itself, would probably not be significantly severe, and therefore, that use of force would not be reasonable.

Although *Graham* has been the law of the land since the Court rendered its decision in 1989, it was not immediately understood or taught by the police. Police agencies were still teaching when to use physical force or their hands, when to use a mechanical control device (such as a baton), and when to use a firearm. These were akin to a checklist that police officers learned to manipulate in their heads when confronting a suspect. Force continuums were taught and based on the suspect's actions and what the corresponding appropriate police reactions should be.

I have seen all kinds of force continuum illustrations in my career, and they all work mostly the same. They are a pyramid of building blocks with numbers or intertwined circles. They are typically multicolored in green, yellow, orange, red, and black to reinforce the danger points. They are training aids used to demonstrate officers' levels of force in response to actions of a subject, and all comprise the same basic road map. To use them, you identify the level of force presented against the officer and then move horizontally or vertically to determine which level of force should be the officer's appropriate response. For example, if a subject is verbally noncompliant during an arrest, the officer would follow the continuum one level above, which indicates the officer may use physical force to gain compliance. If the subject begins to resist physically, go back to the continuum, which indicates the use of a mechanical device, such as a baton, to gain compliance. If the person produces a weapon, such as a knife or a gun, go back to the chart and see that deadly force may be appropriate. Eventually, continuums went the way of the dinosaurs for most agencies, and we generally refrained from using them as teaching aides.

In about 2003, a few talented instructors at the FLETC developed a new use-of-force teaching philosophy. I was privileged to be stationed there and was present for early briefings on the new curriculum. They began teaching the use of force applying the Fourth Amendment, sans the continuum model. Their theory, a sound one, was if the Court ruled in *Graham* that all police force applications should be judged based upon the reasonableness standard of the Fourth Amendment, we should be teaching it that way. They concluded that the multicolored continuum with levels, steps, and colors created confusion among the use-of-force decision-makers, the police. It was likely contributing to officer safety risks because it required officers to manipulate a time-consuming and complicated decision-making process in "tense, uncertain, and rapidly evolving circumstances."[9]

The FLETC developed this new and innovative teaching methodology and rolled it out in their new Use-of-Force Instructor Training Program (UOFITP). As the use-of-force representative from my agency, I saw it as a fresh look at use-of-force training. It incorporated classroom case analysis and practical, reality-based, teach-back exercises. This training program quickly became one of the FLETC's most sought-after continuing education courses and remains so to this day, which is a credit to its designers.

I sent several of my firearms instructors to the program. One of the first few students I sent came to me shortly afterward with an observation that concerned me. This highly talented firearms instructor told me that to him everything had changed in use of force. That troubled me because nothing had changed. The only thing that the FLETC changed was the teaching methodology. Was this an indication that new law enforcement students going through the academy, and subsequent annual in-services, did not have an understanding of the Fourth Amendment as it applied to the use of force? Were students learning it well enough to pass an exam but not effectively enough to learn its application in a use-of-force event? If this highly talented student thought everything in use of force was different, we needed to do a better job teaching it.

Unfortunately, I believe that although it has been almost twenty years since we introduced that revolutionary use-of-force teaching methodology, we continue to lack a real understanding of the Fourth Amendment. Part of the reason is that we teach the use of force in a vacuum. We send people to the UOFITP, and the entire focus of the Fourth Amendment instruction relates to use of force by the police. The reality is, nowhere in those fifty-four words is the word "force" used. The Fourth Amendment is about people. It is about the protection of people from the unreasonableness of government. If we go back to the Court, we recall that the justices told us that the reasonableness of all police use of force is evaluated by the reasonableness standard of the Fourth Amendment. Yet, we teach it as a use-of-force issue and not as a constitutional guarantee.

Most law enforcement officers receive use-of-force training at least once a year. The training usually includes a review of the department's use-of-force policy and relevant case law, mainly the big three as we like to call them: *Graham v. Connor, Tennessee v. Garner,* and *Scott v. Harris.* Most police departments' use-of-force policies include these cases as the framework for their policies and train on the objective reasonableness language in each. Some policies go even further and set forth specific prohibitions or requirements not identified in these cases. These include not permitting warning shots and prohibiting officers from shooting at moving vehicles when the vehicle is the only weapon present.

I taught these classes many times a year and would typically begin the course with an analysis of *Delaware v. Prouse*.[10] This is a favorite of mine because once I learned it early in my career, it forced me to change my patrol techniques. Essentially, the Court held that police need a reason to stop a car, and the practice of merely making a car stop to check for license and registration is a Fourth Amendment seizure and unreasonable. In nearly every class, a veteran agent would question my old-age senility and remind me that we were supposed to be talking about the use of force and *Graham*. No one ever heard of *Delaware v. Prouse*, but they were about to learn it.

I also incorporated *Terry v. Ohio*,[11] and the responses were similar. In *Terry*, the Court held that an investigative stop, even if brief, was a seizure, and its legitimacy had to be weighed against the Fourth Amendment reasonableness standard. Again, a veteran special agent would raise his or her hand and challenge me that *Terry v. Ohio* dealt with investigative stops, not use of force. On days when I felt particularly mischievous, I continued my legal analysis, which I would quip was practicing law without a license and included in the discussion my all-time favorite Supreme Court case: *Katz v. United States*.[12] It was decided in 1967, and it is the quintessential case that affirmed the Fourth Amendment reasonableness standard. Their eyes would roll into the back of their heads and with good reason. *Katz* was the fundamental case taught in Fourth Amendment classes at the FLETC's CITP. There were numerous, complicated test questions dealing with *Katz* that a CITP student had to master. Lectures on *Katz* were part of the Fourth Amendment instruction that dealt with searches, not police use of force.

Jim Baker drummed *Katz* into my head and assured me that if

I understood it, and the reasonable expectation of privacy (REP), I could apply reasonableness to any situation. The Court held that people have a reasonable expectation of privacy and that any police intrusion of that privacy must be reasonable. Katz entered a phone booth and had a conversation on the phone about illegal activity. The police had installed a listening device on the outside of the phone booth to listen and record Katz's conversations. Arguably, one could hear Katz's side of the conversation outside the phone booth if the door was open. However, Katz closed the door, and at that point, he reasonably demonstrated he wanted privacy for his conversation. The police needed to overcome Katz's REP in order to obtain a court order to listen to his conversation. They did not and therefore were not reasonable when monitoring Katz's private telephone call.

I raised these Supreme Court cases, not to confuse students, but to engage them in a different approach to use-of-force analysis. Questions about my choice of case law confirmed my suspicions that many police officers still did not understand the essence of the Fourth Amendment and, more specifically, how it applies to the use of force. To this day, officers are likely to tell us that they either searched or seized a person for officer safety or because they were in fear of bodily harm. Nowhere in those fifty-four words does that reasoning appear, but officers draw that conclusion and thus attempt to justify a Fourth Amendment intrusion.

The fifty-four words of the Fourth Amendment are about the protection of people against unreasonable actions by the government. The key word here is *people*. The police are responsible for ensuring that all actions against people, including the use of force, are reasonable. There is no other government representative with authority to decide reasonableness and take actions consistent with the reasonableness that may result in taking a life. Police have the sole authority to seize a person. It is an awesome responsibility that comes with serious accountability. The prohibitions against unreasonableness are very severe and require the police to satisfy a considerable standard of proof, yet the Court interpreted reasonableness without a hard and fast rule. The Court used the words "tense," "uncertain" and "rapidly evolving" to define a situation when police can use force.

That analysis is very different from examining reasonableness for purposes of issuing a search warrant. In those instances, there is time for thought and decision-making. Further, the totality of the circumstances does not usually give rise to tense, uncertain, and rapidly evolving events that define use-of-force situations. For searches, the Court continues to reaffirm that all searches without a warrant are, on their face, unreasonable. There is time to examine facts and present those facts as probable cause to a judicial authority that can issue a warrant to search. In the absence of a warrant, the police need to overcome the assumption that the search was unreasonable. That is a very different application of the same constitutional standard of reasonableness applicable in police use of force.

The Court gave the police much latitude in these tense, uncertain, and rapidly evolving use-of-force events and chose not to judge the actions of the officer with twenty-twenty hindsight. The Court avoids examining actions the officer could have chosen and instead evaluates the actions the officer chose. In 2007, the Court demonstrated this analysis in *Scott v Harris*.[13]

In *Scott v. Harris*, Officer Scott attempted to stop (seize) Harris for driving seventy-three miles per hour (mph) in a fifty-five-mph zone. Although minor in its intrusiveness, the stop needed to be reasonable. However, Harris failed to stop, accelerated his speed, and Scott pursued him. Harris reached speeds above one hundred miles per hour during the pursuit. Eventually, Scott initiated a pursuit intervention technique (PIT) with his patrol car, which worked to stop Harris (seizure). The PIT resulted in Harris losing control of his car, crashing, and sustaining lifelong debilitating injuries. Harris alleged that the police violated his Fourth Amendment protections against unreasonable seizures because Scott's use of force in the stop was unreasonable. Harris asserted that he would have slowed to a safe speed and stopped had the officer ceased his pursuit of him. The Court first determined that the PIT was, in fact, a Fourth Amendment seizure. The Court then evaluated the seizure against Harris' claim that it was unreasonable and his assertion that he would have slowed down and stopped if the police stopped pursuing him. Although the Court did not discount Harris' claims, it indicated that the police could not be expected to project or evaluate what Harris might do in the future. It determined that at the moment Scott initiated the seizure (by the PIT), Harris's speed and manner of driving were a threat to the community and other officers, he was attempting to evade arrest by flight, and therefore, the seizure was reasonable. The Court was clear. It would not examine a police use-of-force decision based upon what other options the police could have employed but rather would determine the reasonableness of the options they did employ. Based upon the totality of the circumstances, the Court determined that Scott was reasonable in his seizure of Harris.

Tennessee v. Garner is the third of the big three Supreme Court decisions that apply to police use of force that officers are taught in the police academy and throughout their careers. *Tennessee*, like *Graham* and *Scott*, was decided well after I became a police officer. These decisions were rendered several years into my career, and their effects on the evolution of policing are valuable lessons for today's officers. When they became the law, we all needed to change the way we policed. Policing in and of itself did not change. We continued to do our jobs, but the way we did our jobs did change. That is an important distinction. Changing the way we police, not changing policing, is a central theme of this book.

We teach the Court's decision in *Tennessee v. Garner* out of order. The Court decided *Graham* in 1989, four years after *Tennessee v. Garner*. So why do we teach *Graham* first? Ask a law enforcement officer what *Tennessee v. Garner* is about, and the officer is likely to say it is about deadly force. They remember it that way because that is the way we teach it. Most use-of-force law enforcement instruction starts with *Graham v. Connor* and then moves to either *Tennessee v. Garner* or *Scott v. Harris*. However, *Tennessee v. Garner* is the first case that deals with the reasonableness of the police in use of force. Police will indicate that *Graham* is about objective reasonableness, *Tennessee* is about deadly force, and *Scott* reinforces the *Graham* objective reasonableness standard. That is not entirely wrong, but the analysis is incomplete. All of these Supreme Court decisions are Fourth Amendment cases about people and the protection of people against unreasonable government seizures. The manner and order we teach them are as problematic as our old, multicolored, step force continuum.

We are teaching officers to think objective reasonableness and then deadly force. It is all about the reasonableness requirement of the Fourth Amendment—no matter the force applied. I have read each of these Supreme Court cases, including the dissenting opinions. One cannot help but identify the tone of these opinions as the Court affirms its position in *Tennessee* and reaffirms it in *Graham* and *Scott*. That is, the use of force by the police must be judged based on the Fourth Amendment standard of reasonableness. This case law and the evolution of the Court's thinking is remarkable to read, and I highly suggest it for all use-of-force students.

The Court decided *Tennessee v. Garner*[14] in 1985. For much of my career, we taught different levels of force—physical, mechanical, and deadly. Each of these required an officer to meet a standard in order to apply them. Deadly, the most serious application of force, was presented as a specific learning objective. I learned specific instances when I could use deadly force in 1978 at the New Jersey State Police Academy and even before that in 1973 at the United States Air Force Security Police Academy. I learned that deadly force was my last option and was only authorized after I exhausted all other force applications. There were also specific instances that authorized the use of deadly force. Burglary of an occupied dwelling, for instance, was a specific circumstance when deadly force was authorized. The test questions were straightforward and merely required the learner to memorize the instances when deadly force was authorized. That instruction was, in part, the basis for the facts later examined by the Court in *Tennessee*.

The police suspected Garner of committing a residential burglary in Memphis, Tennessee. The police arrived at the scene and observed a subject (Garner) fleeing the area by running through the backyard and attempting to climb a fence to escape. The law in Tennessee authorized deadly force if police met with resistance or a demonstration of flight to avoid arrest. Also, the department policy specifically authorized deadly force for a burglary. Police officers, based on this authority and the circumstances, fired on Garner. They struck him in the back and killed him as he climbed a fence. Garner's father alleged that the police violated his son's constitutional rights and filed an action against the police. The Court's decision provided important guidance for police use of force. The Court notably found that all seizures by the police, including seizures with a firearm or bullet, are in fact seizures. The Court further held that, as such, these seizures must be examined based upon their reasonableness as required by the Fourth Amendment and not a state statute indicating specific instances when deadly force is authorized. Justice White delivered the opinion of the Court and said,

> This case requires us to determine the constitution-
> ality of the use of deadly force to prevent the escape
> of an apparently unarmed suspected felon. We con-
> clude that such force may not be used unless it is
> necessary to prevent the escape and the officer has
> probable cause to believe that the suspect poses a
> significant threat of death or serious physical injury
> to the officer or others.

The use of deadly force to prevent the escape of felony suspects, whatever the circumstances, is constitutionally unreasonable. It is not better that felony suspects die rather than that they escape. Where the suspect poses no immediate threat to the officer and no threat to others, the harm resulting from failing to apprehend him does not justify the use of deadly force to do so. It is no doubt unfortunate when a suspect who is in sight escapes, but the fact that the police arrive a little late or are a little slower afoot does not always justify killing the suspect. A police officer may not seize an unarmed, non-dangerous suspect by shooting him dead. The Tennessee statute is unconstitutional insofar as it authorizes the use of deadly force against such fleeing suspects.[15]

It is not, however, unconstitutional on its face. Where the officer has probable cause to believe that the suspect poses a threat of serious physical harm, either to the officer or to others, it is not constitutionally unreasonable to prevent escape by using deadly force. Thus, if the suspect threatens the officer with a weapon or there is probable cause to believe that he has committed a crime involving the infliction or threatened infliction of serious physical harm, deadly force may be used if necessary, to prevent escape, and if, where feasible, some warning has been given. As applied in such circumstances, the Tennessee statute would pass constitutional muster.[16]

I have been both a teacher and a learner of use-of-force concepts for many years. Use-of-force lesson plan teaching points include the application of the Fourth Amendment reasonableness standard in all use-of-force events, including potentially deadly ones. However, what is often lacking is a thorough examination of the word "necessary," a word repeated throughout the Court's opinion. We once taught deadly force as the last option of the police, and it was only applicable within the parameters of the law. Although we do not teach the use of force like that anymore, we could argue that the word "necessary" used by the Court is similar to the words "last resort," which were a part of the common law doctrine we taught for many years.

When reading *Tennessee v. Garner*, the word "necessary" continues to hit you square in the face. The Court opined that not all force applications need to be deadly. We do not need to kill everyone we arrest, but sometimes it is necessary. Whether or not that seizure by killing is lawful needs to be judged against the Fourth Amendment application of reasonableness. The Court was very clear about the need to protect people against unreasonable seizures and that seizures made with deadly force must be both reasonable and necessary.

Sometimes we forget the word "necessary." I never second-guess an officer-involved shooting. When someone asks my opinion about an officer's decision to use force, I always answer, "It depends." It is a decision that an officer makes when he believes it to be reasonable in a tense, uncertain, and rapidly evolving situation based upon the totality of the circumstances at the time the force was applied.

Rarely does a week go by that we do not hear about a police use-of-force incident involving anything from physical force, a Taser, or an officer-involved shooting. The commonness among these is that they involve action by the police that is an intrusion on a person. When the police use force, it is usually determined to be reasonable—even when we morally do not agree with it. Even more than morally not agreeing with it, we do not like it. We do not agree or like it because we are focused on our morality of right and wrong, but right and wrong is not the standard. Neither are our likes and dislikes. Police use of force is about an intrusion of people's rights and whether that intrusion was reasonable. Police use of force is about the Fourth Amendment, and that is about people.

The evening before sending men to die on the beaches of Normandy, General Eisenhower, upon being briefed on the limiting weather conditions, is purported to have said, "I do not like it, but there it is." The general did not like what he needed to do, and people died as a result of his decision, but it was necessary. History proved that his decisions, although disliked, were the correct ones. Officer-involved shootings are often like that. We do not like to see people shot or officers involved in shootings, but sometimes it happens because it is necessary. Subsequent evaluations of these uses of force are often shown to be reasonable—even the ones we do not like.

Some people may say that we if grudgingly agree with a legal analysis that makes the shooting of an unarmed person reasonable, it is time to change the United States Constitution. That may be true. Perhaps twenty-first-century America is changing—and so should policing. However, we need to keep in mind that the Constitution has been around for more than two hundred years. It is not perfect, but its longevity proves that the authors knew what they were doing when they wrote it.

CHAPTER TWO

PREJUDICE, RACISM, AND BIAS COPS

When I was a kid, there were plenty of jokes about vegetables and specifically about Brussels sprouts. I can still hear the television sitcom moms telling their kids to eat Brussels sprouts. Not one TV kid liked Brussels sprouts. We ate them at my house because that was the way it was, and I liked the way my mom made them. I would never admit liking Brussels sprouts to another kid though, because that was not normal.

Chapter 2
Prejudiced, Racist, and Biased Cops

The word *racist* continues to get thrown around in the political arena. The last presidential election elevated it to a new level, and the most recent midterms succeeded in keeping it there. The next election will likely exceed all expectations of just how high or low we can go in dividing our people.

Cops do not think they are racist or prejudiced or biased. We are not naïve. Some are. Those who are chose the wrong profession. If we find them among our ranks, we need to correct any objectionable behavior or remove them from our agencies. Getting rid of a racist cop may not be easy, but that should not prevent us from doing what is necessary. The police do difficult but necessary things almost every day. It is our normal.

There are cops with varying degrees of bias in today's police departments. However, consider the effect of bias on fair-minded policing in its strictest sense. Cops see the best people at their worst and the worst people at their best. They respond to the homes of the most respected members of the community to mediate domestic quarrels, and they observe firsthand the ugliness in people. They also see people with little means helping someone worse off than they are. To a cop, his opinion is formed by the reality of what is happening at the moment—not by what might be or what was. It just depends.

The subject that police had to fight the last time they arrested

him could act that way again, or the subject could be fully coopera-
tive. It just depends. If there is a bias at all in policing, it is about the
differences between the police and everyone else. Cops are guilty of
being biased toward other cops and biased against people in general,
which comes from the cynicism ingrained in policing. I write about
this in a later chapter in this book. More difficult than cynicism is
addressing implicit bias, which we often do not recognize.

In October 2017, the International Association of Chiefs of
Police (IACP) held their annual installation of officers' dinner in
Philadelphia. Louis M. Dekmar, chief of the LaGrange, Georgia,
Police Department, was being installed as the incoming IACP
president. In his inauguration speech, Chief Dekmar described the
apology given by his town to the African American citizens of his
community for inequality their ancestors experienced. Listening to
the chief's comments, it resonated that this was an example of a police agency doing what it could to engage its community. It is likely
that Chief Dekmar and the elected officials of LaGrange personally
had nothing to apologize for, but that was not the point. The point
was that he was acknowledging wrongs that occurred by the police.
Over the years, I have heard similar stories of the mistreatment of
large populations. Japanese Americans in the United States during
World War II are just one example. There is often a reluctance by
people or groups to apologize, even symbolically, for things that
happened outside of their purview or responsibility. Chief Dekmar
demonstrated that the existing government had a responsibility to
acknowledge the long-ago mistreatment of its people.[17]

The apology was powerful and is an example of the kind of
leadership we need in policing today. It is the kind of leadership
we see in police executives like the former commissioner of the
Philadelphia Police Department, Charles Ramsey, who is a cop's
cop. Commissioner Ramsey, during a recent interview, stated that
the issue is not merely officer-involved shootings of young black
men, but it is also about the young black men who are dying from

gun violence across America. It is about all people dying from gun violence.

Those two men are not anomalies. They are not indicative of every chief, but they are not as rare as they may have been just a few short years ago. Police departments are getting it. They understand that while they might not be doing anything wrong, they can still be better. They understand that they may be legally justified in what they are doing, but they are asking if they can safely do it differently. Every police executive who demonstrates this kind of leadership is a career police officer. They are not politicians. They are not social workers. They are cops. Like General Douglas MacArthur reportedly said, "The soldier above all other people prays for peace, for he must suffer and bear the deepest wounds and scars of war." Every professional police officer also prays for peace in their cities and towns because it is the cop who experiences firsthand the tragedy of violence.

As a white man who grew up in a rural, primarily white community in the fifties and sixties, I know that implicit bias is a part of me. The bias is not visible, but it is indeed there. Elementary school was not quite in one room, but it was close. Every kid in the class was pretty much the same and white. As the grades progressed, so too did the changes in the way kids looked. Somehow, we knew some kids were different than we were and not just by the color of their skin. I have no idea why they were different than I was, and I do not know how I knew it. I acquired these thoughts from the culture that surrounded me. I do not know if the adults around me were racists, but they used language that is indicative of racism. Gradually I began to recognize a division. It did not just stop there. Differences in daily news reports, other media, and even cartoons accentuated these differences. I did not grow up in the South where the differences openly involved blacks and whites. I grew up in the North where the differences were also among Christians and Jews, Catholics and Protestants, Asians, the Irish, Puerto Ricans, and Italians.

The differences in people and any associated biases were not just about skin color, ethnicity, or religion. Hairstyles, music preferences, and manner of dress all became the subjects of likes, dislikes, differences, and opinions that contributed to the biases of that time. Some of the hairstyles, music, and manner of dress of the 1960s portrayed a drug-using draft dodger who burned the flag. It was those people, and we knew who those people were. They were the different ones.

The first recollection I have of organized violence with a race connection was in 1968. I was in junior high school. One day, a few boys got into a fight. Some were black, and some were white. I did not know why they were fighting, but I remember watching the evening news that night and seeing rioting across America. I soon figured out that the black kids in school were on one side of the issue, and my friends and I were on the other. We were not active participants in the violence, but somehow we knew we were supposed to be on the side of the white kids. These observations, together with the comments that I heard at home and from other adults, did a pretty fair job of reinforcing the differences I later learned were prejudices. I cannot do anything about my upbringing, what I experienced as a young person, or what I was exposed to. I can only be aware of its impact on me and what I can do to alter its influences.

America's unrest at that time was more than racial. We talk about the country being divided today like never before, and there is some truth to that. However, in 1968, the news was all about people demonstrating against the war in Vietnam and burning draft cards and the American flag. The news was full of these protests, and the cops were in helmets, carrying riot sticks, and firing tear gas into crowds. At Kent State University, the Ohio National Guard fired live ammunition into the demonstrators.[18] Violence consumed us in the late 1960s. We were fighting communists in Vietnam, and it seemed as though we were fighting a war among ourselves in the United States as well. Many of our young men died in Vietnam. In April 1968, Dr. Martin Luther King was murdered, and two months later, so was Robert F. Kennedy. America was divided, and the police were at the epicenter of that divide.

I have been to dozens of in-service trainings that centered on understanding bias and diversity. Some of these were mandatory and usually because something went wrong or my agency was part of a lawsuit. Some of these were voluntary, and I chose to attend for my personal growth. I wanted to be a better supervisor, a better crisis peer supporter, a better police instructor, and a better person. I realized that understanding how bias affects us can help to de-escalate a violent encounter and help keep my officers and members of the public safe. To me, this was powerful.

Some of the biases that were a part of my early upbringing are no longer a part of who I am. Some of the things I may have done that had their origins in bias I no longer do. Let us not jump to any conclusions that I am a reformed white supremacist or something similar. It was and is not that overt. My parents were not phobic racists. My parents were average white people raised during the Great Depression. My mother remembered her family's small farm being foreclosed on by the bank. She remembered her and her brothers and sisters being hungry. None of this had anything to do with the color of skin; poverty is truly color-blind. They retained a lifetime mistrust of banks and supported Democrats for the rest of their lives because Franklin Delano Roosevelt was one, and he got the country out of the Great Depression.

Some of my biases may not be completely gone. Although I cannot change that any more than I can the color of the hair I once had, I can consciously chose not to allow them to interfere with my behavior. However, these biases are only the obvious ones I have identified and acknowledged. They do not account for the ones I am not consciously aware of that could manifest themselves in a high-stress encounter. How is the implicit bias that I cannot identify, even though I know it exists, going to affect my decisions in that tense, uncertain, and rapidly evolving event?

Implicit bias is much subtler than racism and more challenging to identify and fix. The Kirwan Institute at Ohio State University defined implicit bias:

> The attitudes or stereotypes that affect our understanding, actions, and decisions in an unconscious manner. These biases, which encompass both favorable and unfavorable assessments, are activated involuntarily and without an individual's awareness or intentional control. Residing deep in the subconscious, these biases are different from known biases that individuals may choose to conceal for the purposes of social and/or political correctness. Rather, implicit biases are not accessible through introspection. The implicit associations we harbor in our subconscious cause us to have feelings and attitudes about other people based on characteristics such as race, ethnicity, age, and appearance. These associations develop over the course of a lifetime beginning at a very early age through exposure to direct and indirect messages. In addition to early life experiences, the media and news programming are often-cited origins of implicit associations."[19]

Implicit bias can be in the person who has nothing consciously against people who are not like him, but he feels uncomfortable getting too close to them. It can be the homeowner with new neighbors who are different and cause her concern. Is it an aversion to interpersonal contact with strangers? Is it bias? Is it both? What about the cop who makes a stop and does not realize the role implicit bias plays in his actions? Did he improperly profile the driver and stop him, or was it unconsciously contributory? There are also people of color in America who mistrust the police and suspect that they are being stopped for DWB (driving while black) even though they are committing a known traffic violation.

Implicit bias is seen in Gregory Peck's Philip Schuyler Green character in the movie *Gentlemen's Agreement.*[20] He learns that it is not enough to not overtly participate in discrimination, but it requires one to call it out when it is wrong. Someone with implicit bias may not participate in the disparaging racial, religious, and sexual orientation conversations but does nothing to stop them either. If we have learned nothing else, we know that racism and bias do not need to be fueled to survive. They will thrive in the silence of people doing nothing about it.

Retired, Alcohol, Tobacco and Firearms (ATF) Special Agent (SA) Matthew Horace in his excellent book, *The Black and The Blue,*[21] writes a lot about racism and implicit bias. He experienced it as a black man, as a black cop, and as a cop. There is a difference. SA Horace does a great job pointing out the differences. His book continues to be a part of my ever-evolving education on the subject. It should be a must-read for every cop of all colors and persuasions.

There is a scene in the movie classic, *Guess Who's Coming to Dinner*[22] that depicts what SA (ret.) Horace writes about in his book. Sidney Poitier's character, Dr. John Prentice, tells his father that he sees himself as a black man, but Prentice sees himself as a man. I appreciate what Prentice was saying because it is analogous to the view I have when I see a cop. I see blue. I do not see skin color, and I think most cops think that way. The teaching point is beyond black, white, and blue. We see people when we see people and not the color of their skin, their culture, or their ethnicity.

There was a headline recently about a bill pending in the New Hampshire legislature. The headline essentially said that the bill was going to prohibit New Hampshire police officers from using deadly force. It generated many pro-police comments about the unfairness of such a bill. I decided to read the bill and discovered that it does not say that at all. There is no intent to prohibit the police from using deadly force when it is necessary. The bill, as written, seeks to remove the word *arrest* as an element in which deadly force can be used, but it retains the elements of reasonableness that the Court identified in *Tennessee v. Garner.*[23]

Why did the headline quickly generate all of those opinions? The answer lies, at least in part, in bias. There are more than a few law enforcement groups that believe their ability to police is being encroached on by legislatures, the department of justice, and the courts. There may be some factual basis for this, but they are not entirely accurate. On the other hand, there is a segment of society who believe the police are out of control and any attempt to limit police power is a good thing. This proposed law, as reported, purported to do that. Both of these positions are, at least in part, rooted in bias and misinformation or, at a minimum, incomplete information that furthers the inaccuracies of bias.

The divide we have in this country between pro and anti-police is as wide as it has ever been. The blue lives matter movement responds in opposition to the black lives matter movement. The police are called murderers by some and warriors and heroes by others. The headlines with incomplete information do nothing to lessen these differences. Instead, they widen them. The people who hate cops and want their ability to use force limited are cheering the bill while the cops are reeling in anger from more stringent laws that make their job more dangerous. The bill does neither, but the rhetoric broadens the division and continues to enforce the bias. The false reality feeds on the bias that is already there.

It is easy to join like-minded people in a cause without validating the reality of it, but it is irresponsible and further divides us as a people. It is more than divisive though. It is also dangerous. Every major shooting we see in this country is typically a result of an unbalanced or misguided person who chose an extreme solution to some cause. Assassins are murdering cops in their patrol cars for the same reasons. There is no reality testing of their cause. They believe in what they are doing. Some may say that those examples are different from some of the other debates on guns, politics, and policing. The truth is that there is very little difference. It is about mistrust, hate, and anger. It is happening every day in America.

I recently attended a dinner party with a few people, none of whom were in law enforcement. Someone told a story about being stopped by a cop. I have heard these stories a thousand times, and they inevitably come up at these kinds of gatherings. I genuinely wish I had a quarter for every time I have had to listen to somebody tell me their police story. I would be a wealthy man. The conversation evolved into the deterioration of America and its causes. He said that police violence was so prevalent because people do not listen to what the police tell them to do. Police call this a failure to comply. This person opined that people should merely obey police commands, and it would result in less violence. He supported his assertion with his own successful stories about police stops of past middle-aged, white people. He had a strong opinion that if we merely allow the police to do their job, everything would be fine. The opinions reminded me of a book I read by D. L. Hughley: *How Not to Get Shot*.[24] I enjoyed reading that book, but these comments were irritating. They were irritating because too many people are dying in our streets. Some are cops, and some are not. It is not a game out there, and to simplify it the way he did made it seem so inconsequential.

I do not know if people around me think they have to voice their opinions about the police because they think it is what I want to hear or because they genuinely believe them. It is probably a little of both. I listened for a while, and I validated his opinions where I could, but there came the point when I had to correct the rhetoric. When the conversation turned to Ferguson, Missouri, and the shooting of Michael Brown by Officer Darren Wilson, I had to correct him.[25]

He knew that the black man (whose name he did not know) had just robbed a store. He also knew, or thought he knew, that the cop (whose name he did not know) shot the subject who matched the description of the robber when he resisted arrest and tried to get away. He concluded that the officer would not have shot the subject (Brown) if he had obeyed the police. I could have validated his misinformation, but because I believe in what I am writing about in this book, I had to set the record straight.

Some strongly believe that Officer Darren Wilson is responsible for Michael Brown's death. There is also a strong opinion that Michael Brown's actions resulted in his death. My only conclusion about that shooting is that Michael Brown should not be dead. I do not assign culpability for his death because it is much more complicated than that. One of the things I hope you are learning from this book is that hindsight opinions of police actions are irrelevant to their reasonableness. More importantly, when those opinions are based on mistaken or incorrect information, they further contribute to the deterioration of the relationships the police are trying to build.

I recently read an editorial about a cop who was off-duty with his family and came upon a serious motor vehicle accident. One of the vehicles was burning, and there was a gasoline leak. The off-duty officer reacted to the event, removed the lone occupant from the burning car, and arguably saved her life. The woman later wrote a letter to the officer's chief complaining about his appearance. She was explicitly offended by several of the officer's tattoos and wrote the chief that the officer looked like a monster. The woman concluded that this type of man should not be a police officer. She did not reference any other description of the officer such as size or facial hair. She rested her conclusion solely on his tattoos, which she found to be menacing. I do not know anything about this woman and cannot offer an opinion about her perception of the officer as a monster. I suspect though, that either a learned or cultural indoctrination, or both, contributed to her opinion that the officer looked menacing.

I personally do not like tattoos, especially the ones that depict graphics that I associate with violence. I do not like facial hair, especially the circle beard or goatee that is so prevalent on men today, and I do not like full beards either. I do not like shaved heads even though I shave mine. I especially do not like a bald, tattooed, large- or small-framed white guy with a round beard. That leaves men of medium frame, average looks, clean-shaven, and combed hair. Are these likes or dislikes important, and if so, why? What is it that I do not like about that bald, tattooed, large- or small-framed white guy with the round beard? Even more, why does that look produce some fear in me? Where does that come from—and how did I make that association? It probably came, in part, from the clean-shaven, combed hair, and overall clean-cut appearance that was my normal growing up.

My father was retired military, and that is the way it was around our house. The clean-cut look was the norm. Hair was cut short or at least shorter than everyone else. My father had short hair and was clean-shaven every day of his life. Whatever was not my normal was different, and differences morphed into dislikes. I know these biases exist in me. Not long ago, I was teaching a use-of-force class to agents. The discussion centered on appearance and how they should present themselves to security personnel in airports. During the presentation I used the term *clean-cut*, and not one student knew what it meant. I immediately recognized it, and at the same time, I was surprised that it came out of my mouth so easily from all those years ago.

I wonder why brussels sprouts have become such a favorite vegetable. When I was a kid, there were plenty of jokes about vegetables and specifically about brussels sprouts. I can still hear the television sitcom moms telling their kids to eat their brussels sprouts. Not one TV kid liked brussels sprouts. We ate them at my house because that was the way it was, and I liked the way my mom made them. I would never admit liking brussels sprouts to another kid though because that was not normal. Somehow the bias against brussels sprouts disappeared over the years because everyone likes them now, especially shaved and roasted with bacon. I guess it took some creative advertising to overcome the bias against brussels sprouts.

Racism—admitted or acknowledged—and implicit biases are real, and they can be a significant problem for the police. A racist person who joins the cops has entered the wrong profession and needs to be fired. End of story. Implicit bias is more challenging, but it can be corrected.

The first thing that has to happen is to acknowledge that implicit bias exists. It is there even if we cannot see it or identify it. That is hard for a cop. A cop's whole livelihood, and for that matter life, depends on the reality of what is. Cops need to identify things. They do not operate well in altered realities so discussions about implicit bias need to make sense. We need to be able to define bias so officers can relate to it and understand it. It may be hard for some to recognize it, but like probable cause, we need to know it when we see it. If we can accept that it exists and recognize it when we see it, we can do something about it. I believe good cops can recognize it and make appropriate corrections in the way they deal with people. They do it every day, but it is also important to know why they are doing it.

Implicit bias is not something we work to achieve or something we knowingly teach ourselves. It is an accumulation of things we have been exposed to, thought about, and experienced. Together, they shape the way we view, interpret, and think. They often become the norm in our lives. Bias can affect how we act on a given stimulus such as a pedestrian stop. The Ohio State University Kirwan Institute for the Study of Race and Ethnicity describes it as follows:

A Few Key Characteristics of Implicit Biases

- Implicit biases are pervasive. Everyone possesses them, even people with avowed commitments to impartiality such as judges.

- Implicit and explicit biases are related but distinct mental constructs. They are not mutually exclusive and may even reinforce each other.
- The implicit associations we hold do not necessarily align with our declared beliefs or even reflect stances we would explicitly endorse.
- We generally tend to hold implicit biases that favor our own in-group, though research has shown that we can still hold implicit biases against our in-group.
- Implicit biases are malleable. Our brains are incredibly complex, and the implicit associations we have formed can be gradually unlearned through a variety of debiasing techniques.[26]

Why did that cop stop subject A rather than subject B? The answer to that sergeant test question relates directly to *Terry v. Ohio.* She stopped subject A based upon the observable events that led her to believe that criminal activity was afoot. What were those observable events? What did she see? She probably based her conclusions on conduct she observed that was similar to previous conduct consistent with criminal activity. Implicit bias could have been at work in this situation and could have contributed to the officer's decision. Would another officer, with distinctly different life experiences than this officer, come to the same conclusion? Maybe not, and if not, is it because he does not share the same implicit bias?

When we talk about implicit bias in policing, we often think of a white officer who conducts a *Terry* stop on a black man rather than a white man. Did race affect the officer's decision to stop the person—or were there other relevant factors, such as the person's conduct, that aroused the officer's suspicion? Maybe it had nothing to do with skin color. However, it might have, and if officers can self-evaluate their actions and determine that they may have been influenced by bias, that is where the real learning begins.

This does not mean that skin color should never be a part of an officer's decision to make an investigative stop. There may be a legitimate reason that it was a factor. The officer could be looking for a man with a particular skin color. It means that we should be evaluating the circumstances and actions and learning from them. When it comes to bias, we should be both our best teacher and best student. If we recognize bias when we see it, we can acknowledge it and correct it.

A few years ago, I attended a diversity training class taught by a very knowledgeable instructor. He talked about the realities without attempting to be politically correct in a room of white agents and clerical staff. Cops appreciate that and his generated conversation. I felt comfortable with the guy and asked a question that had been bothering me for a while. The question was about stopping white people in predominately black and brown neighborhoods where there are active narcotics sales. Suburban white kids go into the neighborhoods to purchase narcotics. The question was whether it was possible to profile a white person. The instructor chuckled and commented on my courage to ask the question. He explained that the police are not merely stopping white kids. They are stopping people who are demonstrating possible criminal activity, specifically the purchase of narcotics. We agreed that of the people arrested in these scenarios, some are white, and others are nonwhites. The black and white issue and the legitimate need for guarding against using race as a predicate for stops has led us to avoid mentioning race at all. The race of the people stopped in these kinds of arrests is generally not a factor in the stops. Instead, they are facts about the individuals arrested. The race of the people being stopped was not an issue. I was making it one.

We had an outlaw motorcycle gang's chapter headquarters in town for the first few years I was in uniform. We often had contact with the members of this group, and they were mostly all adversarial. Anytime I saw a large white guy with tattoos and chains on a

Harley-Davidson motorcycle, I immediately suspected that he was an outlaw motorcycle gang member. If the rider was wearing club colors, I knew for sure. If not, I could only suspect that he was a club member. He could have been a cop for that matter because there were plenty of cops who rode like that, but that did not cross my mind then. Fueled by implicit bias, my mind went to, "This is a bad guy." That was learned behavior, a bias I had assimilated as a police officer in that department because of the adversarial relationship we had with the outlaw motorcycle gang.

We need to be aware of the biases we pick up along the way, recognize them when we see them, and change the ones that need changing by invalidating them. That is the most effective way to reprogram bias. As long as we continue to validate them, they will remain and become more of a force in our lives. If we invalidate them when we see them, and understand that they are incorrect, they lose their power to manipulate our subconscious. Left unchecked, they will become our autopilot and take us where we do not want to go.

We use reality-based scenario training to prepare officers to react in high-stress situations. We try to create scripts in the officers' minds that are proven to be successful in gaining the edge and surviving that encounter. We know they work, and when the officer trains in that manner, he comes to know they work. The script that contains unwanted implicit bias could have the same effect but not with the results we want. We may be able to minimize citizen complaints, extra baton strikes, and officer-involved shootings if we strive to understand and correct bias. Recognizing bias and correcting our actions that arise from it can positively affect our citizen contacts.

Bias is not all bad, and information that taught us to stay alive should be embraced and should remain a part of our operating systems. The things we learned about visibility in the car during a stop, actions that are typical of a subject who is carrying a firearm, and the real sense of danger that develops are, in part, a result of biases created from our actions in events that have kept us safe. Those we retain.

Some people only want to talk about bias being detrimental—and leave it there. They believe that all people have biases and that it will affect how they do their job. The cop cannot leave it there. Cops need to be professional students, continue to learn, and act on what they learn. This helps keep them safe. Cops cannot hide from issues of bias because it is uncomfortable. Everything a cop does is uncomfortable. Sometimes they get it wrong, but most of the time, they get it right. The police are people just like everybody else. The police are the people, and the people are the police.

CHAPTER THREE
REACTION, FEAR, AND THE EXTENT IT AFFECTS US

We are not talking about hand wrenching terror. However, the brain is telling the officer the hands are not clear, and that could be a problem.

Chapter 3
Reaction, Fear, and the Extent It Affects Us

The Fourth Amendment is about protecting people against unreasonable seizures, and to some extent, the police are the gatekeepers of the protection. If that is true, why do the police appear to act unreasonably, particularly in use-of-force situations? The answer looks simple enough when we see it on video. The police did not need to punch the subject, strike him with a baton, use a Taser, or fire their weapon. Moreover, even if there was justification to do any of that, they should not have thrown so many punches, should have stopped hitting the subject with the baton, or should have only wounded the subject when they shot. The focus shifts from the officer's initial contact and its reasonableness to what the officer ultimately did.

A court recently sentenced former Chicago Police Officer Jason Van Dyke to eighty-one months incarceration for the shooting death of Laquan McDonald. Van Dyke's conviction of second-degree murder and sixteen counts of aggravated assault (one count for each of the rounds Van Dyke fired at McDonald) were the result of an October 2014 shooting.[27]

Some will argue that McDonald, armed with a knife, remained a threat capable of serious bodily injury or death to Van Dyke and other officers. That is a reasonable assertion based upon what we know about people's ability to commit assaults from a considerable distance even after being shot. I write more about reactions and shooting times later in this chapter.

Most of the force used by the police is not unreasonable. Often, they are consistent with the guidance provided to us in the Court's decision in *Graham v. Connor*. However, some uses of force, even the reasonable ones, can be improved upon, and every cop should want to be better.

Sometimes the police are open about their opinions on uses of force by officers and when appropriate, they make candid statements about whether there was, or was not, an overreaction on the part of an officer. Police also say that videos do not show everything—or they make no statement at all. That raises public suspicion. Even when the police take immediate responsibility for an overreaction or excessive use of force, it does not make up for the loss of a loved one. Despite this, if ethnicity or skin color is a factor, public suspicion is magnified. While the police usually act reasonably, the public does not like it. Most of the time, the police do not like it either. Whether reasonable use of force was used or not, police prefer to accomplish their objective without the need for violence.

However, liking something is not the standard we apply to police use of force. The standard is reasonableness. In order to determine reasonableness, we need a complete understanding of what occurs during these events. The fact that a suspect may have been unarmed is not sufficient information to conclude that the cop was wrong, and it is not enough to say he was right. We cannot attribute it all to bias. It is not a factor in every officer-involved shooting of a black man by a white cop. There are many factors in play in a use-of-force situation, and they are all essential to the investigation. There are no unimportant factors in police use of force.

The Chicago police did not release the dashcam video of Van Dyke shooting McDonald for thirteen months, and even then, the release was the result of a court order. All investigations of shootings, particularly those involving officers, are time-consuming. The reason is that, unlike other shootings, the law allows a police officer to use deadly force reasonably, and determining reasonableness can take time. Investigators should take whatever time they need to ensure that a thorough and complete investigation uncovers all the facts—both inculpatory and exculpatory. However, delays, like the one regarding the video, create the perception that the police are hiding something from the public.

Interpersonal confrontation is one of the greatest fears people have, and the police are no different. Again, because they are people. For example, a person is acting in a disorderly manner and is disruptive to other people nearby. The police officer who has to confront this person is probably going to be met with anger because the officer is about to disrupt whatever it is he is intent on doing. These contacts are often confrontational and adversarial and are difficult and uncomfortable for the police. The subject and the police officer may both have elevated levels of anxiety. There are physiological factors at play that will affect both of them. The higher the stakes, circumstances, or repercussions, the higher the level of anxiety for both people.

De-escalation is a broad topic in our discussions about police actions today. People say the cops need more de-escalation training. They need to find alternative ways of using force, and they need to be more tolerant. One of the first things I learned as a police officer was de-escalation. The first patrol sergeant I worked for, Bob Rosiello, modeled it for me. Bob was a Force Reconnaissance Marine who lost a leg to a land mine in Vietnam. He was also an expert in several martial arts. Rarely did Sergeant Rosiello use force. Instead, he reasoned with unreasonable people who were about to be arrested.

Officers have been practicing de-escalation for a long time because it is the most straightforward course of action for us. It is much easier to talk someone into cooperating than it is to roll around on the ground with them. What we were not doing in the past was teaching it well in our academies. For a while, we got caught up teaching the latest and greatest physical control techniques. We forgot that the most effective techniques involve patiently talking to people. Also, any basic police instructor or field training officer will confirm that personal communications skills in young cops coming on the job have diminished. The fact that we now require formal de-escalation training is both desirable and welcomed. However, it is not a new concept in law enforcement. Cops have always used it.

The reasonableness of the police in a use-of-force situation must include a discussion on reaction versus action or the reactionary curve. Some may remember the old California police television shows of the 1950s and 1960s. *Highway Patrol*[28] with Broderick Crawford, *Dragnet*[29] with Jack Webb, and *Adam-12*[30] with Martin Milner are just a few of the early ones. Force was used by the police in almost every episode of these shows. All of the uses of force we watched had one thing in common: The police always reacted to the bad guys and beat them to the punch. The bad guy's gun misfired, he shot and missed, or the cop was faster and better and won the encounter. Unfortunately, it does not work that way on the street. The cop does not always win. The cop will always be behind the curve when reacting to an assailant's attack—always. There are no exceptions.

A basic rule of pursuit driving is not to follow the car in focus because that is futile. At high speeds above one hundred miles per hour, it is impossible to react to the actions of the pursued car. The pursued driver can do things that allow little time for reaction. Instead, the pursuing officer needs to project the road ahead and possible actions before the need to react. The distance traveled is shortened by reading a curve and hitting an apex, not by following the car. The reactionary curve is reduced and becomes more manageable.

If the car analogy does not make sense, think about the football defensive back working a wide receiver, the defense in basketball, or the shift in baseball. Those actions are all designed to read what is likely to happen and act on the event before the need to react to it.

Similarly, if a police officer is able to recognize and act on something (we call them pre-assault indicators) that could be dangerous, before the event occurs, we greatly increase the odds of safety for everyone.

There is an excellent book about staying in front of the reactionary curve that many use-of-force instructors use as a resource. *Left of Bang*[31] by Patrick Van Horne and Jason A. Riley is about the Marine Corps' combat hunter program. It teaches marines and cops to look at their surroundings before the bang, before the shooting, before the event, or in front of the reactionary curve. It teaches you not to react to an event but to find ways to be in front of the event. I highly recommend this book for every cop.

The Federal Bureau of Investigation analyzed felonious assaults against police officers in 2006.[32] As part of the study, officers who had been the targets of assaults and the offenders were interviewed. Important information came out of that study about the officers' actions, the offenders' perceptions of those actions, the offenders' pre-assault indicators, and the circumstances that brought them together. Also important was the author's development of a theory: the deadly mix. The deadly mix referred to the actions of the officer combined with the actions of the offender and the circumstances that brought them together. This deadly mix was fluid because as each of these three dynamics changed, so did the potential outcome. For instance, if an officer who is not exhibiting sound tactics stops an armed subject who is wanted for a serious crime and is facing significant incarceration, the offender may seize the opportunity to overpower the officer and escape. Each of the components—officer, offender, and the circumstances—contributes to the potential for an assault on the officer. We learned from this analysis that if we could alter the one area that we could control, the officer's actions, we could influence the encounter. We developed our use-of-force lesson plans accordingly and applied these influences in our scenario-based training.

Police contacts with offenders produce anxiety in both people.

The officer is trying to figure out what is going on while assessing the dangerousness of the situation. The officer may know little or nothing about the individual who is the focus of the contact. It is a very uncertain situation for the officer. The offender knows what he is wanted for and the crimes he committed, and he is wary about what the officer knows or is going to do. The offender is assessing the officer and may try to escape or assault her. Both the officer and the offender have a degree of anxiety about what is occurring. That anxiety can be very high, especially if the reason for the contact is a serious one.

A domestic dispute, potentially involving the arrest of a batterer, creates high anxiety because of the consequences and embarrassment that will surely follow. The police officer's anxiety increases if there are noted signs of fear and agitation on the part of the batterer. The police will arrest a shoplifter who has had numerous encounters with the police and several active warrants. That arrest will inevitably involve incarceration and a loss of freedom. Therefore, the offender will have anxiety and will likely attempt to either flee from, or fight, the officer. Alternatively, how about the car or pedestrian stop at night by a lone police officer. Further complicating this stop are multiple occupants of the car who do not look or dress like the officer. Consider the level of anxiety present.

The word *fear* does not emote thoughts of confidence or bravery. Most of us associate the word with terror, being scared, or even cowardice. These words do not describe thoughts or emotions that we are proud of or desire. Indeed, these words are not what we expect from a police officer. We want our officers to be brave, not fearful. Fear, in reality, is none of these. Fear is a natural response. It is a part of us that has but one purpose: to help keep us safe. Fear is not the problem, and we could not do anything about it even if it was. The problem is in our management of fear. Unmanaged fear is a problem. Managed fear can be an asset to us if we learn how to use it. The way the brain processes fear and the body's response to it impact how a police officer functions in a use-of-force event. Some of these functions are automatic and, to the untrained, are not easy to control. Uncontrolled, they can become a severe problem for an officer. However, if we learn to embrace fear, it can become an asset to us.

Patrick Sweeney[33] is a modern-day adventurer and motivational speaker who talks about embracing fear, even welcoming it. His exploits around the world captivate many of us, and he does not appear to have a problem with fear. Sweeney appears to be fearless because of all of the remarkable things he has done, which many of us would never even consider. In reality, he is not fearless at all and remarkably is just like the rest of us. Sweeney has fear too. The difference is that he knows how to manage it, and he makes it work for him. I write more about fear later in this chapter.

According to *Psychology Today*, "Fear is a vital response to physical and emotional danger. If people did not feel fear, they could not protect themselves from legitimate threats."[34] The human body has a remarkable self-protection ability. It has evolved, and humans learned to survive and adapt themselves to overcome many maladies. Early in our development, we learned about fear, and it is interesting to examine what the body does with fear when it senses it.

Merriam-Webster defines fear as "an unpleasant often strong emotion caused by anticipation or awareness of danger."[35] We learn to sense fear. Some fear we are born with, and other fear is learned through life experiences. The more experience we have confronting fear, the more we are aware of it, and that knowledge affects our responses to it.

A small child, for instance, is not afraid to insert a toy into an electric receptacle until he experiences an electrical shock. If that happens, the child remembers it and likely becomes fearful of that receptacle. The child learned to avoid at least that receptacle, and he learned about danger. If we place a cover over the receptacle or use a childproof one that is not accessible to the child he receives no shock and has no fear of that receptacle. It is meaningless to him.

The fear in this example is a good thing because, although not the preferred method, it teaches the child not to repeat the behavior. It is the age-old principle that a stimulus produces a response.

Through my training, I learned how fear affects us. The limbic system works with the amygdala and the hippocampus in the brain to recognize and process danger. They help us figure out what is happening and provide some survival responses. When the amygdala detects danger, a chemical called cortisol is released, which helps excite some of our body systems into emergency or protection mode. The hippocampus, through its memory cards, tries to figure out what the amygdala is detecting and whether it is something to worry about. Is it a real threat to our well-being—or can it be disregarded?

Our dog does not have a well-functioning hippocampus. I am not sure if dogs have them at all. Enzo gets afraid and shakes over the strangest things, none of which are threats. He has not figured out that the clothes dryer buzzer is not a threat, and he goes into fear mode every time it sounds.

While the brain is trying to figure out what is going on, we are afraid or anticipating danger. Without conscious thought, we become concerned only about our survival. This remarkable response to perceived danger has its roots in prehistoric man and has continued to evolve through time. Our body tries to fuel itself with oxygenated blood to prepare us for survival. Our heart rates and blood pressure increases, our breathing becomes more intense, and our visual and auditory receptors become focused and acute. In other words, without our conscience understanding of what is going on, and in our most unconscious thoughts, the body is working to keep us safe. The body alerts the systems that may be needed for survival to be ready and disregards body systems that are not necessary for survival at that moment.

There is one more aspect of fear symptoms that needs mentioning. Cops used to talk about a sixth sensory ability that no one else had. We came to believe we were able to sense danger, and that helped us stay safe. All of the old veteran cops told us to pay attention to that sixth sense. We stopped reinforcing this some years ago because, quite frankly, cops were getting hurt and killed. They were sometimes operating too much on a feeling or hunch and disregarding the things that could hurt them. They were a little too sure of themselves and the ability of the sixth sense to protect them.

While we may not have a sixth sense or extrasensory perception, cops (like all people) have fear symptoms. The recognition of danger or fear can produce the real and physical nuances that we recognize as something not quite right. The hair standing up on the back of the neck, the chill or shudder, and increased heart rate or breathing can all be attributable to the body sensing danger. Officers are taught to watch a subject's hands *and* pay attention to everything else that is happening.

All of these instances create a heightened sense of awareness to protect us from harm. However, we can become hyper-focused on the stimuli at the expense of losing sight of other things going on around us. Those same systems that are working to protect us can get in our way and inhibit our ability to make calm, rational decisions. Most of us have heard of fight-or-flight responses. These are a culmination of the fear responses to stimuli that conclude that either we need to flee—or we need to stay around and fight. If we flee, we are not trying to figure out what is causing our fear. We are getting out of there. Watch a deer in the woods sense something out of the ordinary. They do not investigate the cause. They flee. Maybe this is an inappropriate response to a branch breaking from the wind, but it is an effective survival response that keeps the deer safe.

If the other response, fight, is activated, a similar uncontrolled response can occur. The force delivered to the fight can be uncontrolled, irrational, and excessive to the fear event. This release of energy is evident by the spent feeling after only a few seconds of a physical encounter. The body did not keep anything in reserve. It delivered all of its energy to fight off the threat. If the officer has a weapon like a baton, Taser, or even a firearm, the results can be even more dramatic.

Remember, the police are people and react just like every other person in response to fear. The police are taught to focus on those things that can hurt them, and usually this is something in a subject's hands. If the officer cannot see what is in a subject's hands, then a certain amount of fear about the potential for danger could be experienced. We are not talking about hand-wrenching terror. However, the brain is telling the officer that the hands are not clear, and that could be a problem. Listen to any video of a cop trying to control a subject, and you will hear the words, "Let me see (or show me) your hands." Cops want to see the hands because that is where the danger is, and that is what can hurt them. All of the unconscious sympathetic body systems connect to the threat and the need to survive. If the subject shows the officer his hands, and they are empty, the officer can conclude there is nothing that can hurt him. As a result, the fear subsides slightly, and those systems begin to return to normal. Returning those systems to normal is important because it moves us from survival mode to rational thought.

If a subject has her hands in her pockets or her hands are closed or not visible, then the hands have not been cleared—and the subject remains a threat until they are. The officer's fear continues and along with it an escalation of physiological factors that are beyond the officer's control. The brain has not determined whether this danger is a real threat, and it is preparing to survive. Danger and heightened anxiety can become a real problem if the officer has his finger on the trigger of his pistol while all of this is happening.

As the anxiety continues to escalate in both the officer and the offender, the officer's elevated or unclear voice can contribute to physiological responses happening during the event. If the offender's anxiety is high, her auditory receptors could be minimizing the officer's verbal commands or be focusing more on something else. The result in these dangerous situations is that the officer is ordering the subject to do something that may not be audible, or even worse, can be confusing to the offender. Due to what is occurring in the offender's brain, it is likely that he does not hear or understand what the officer is saying.

We routinely see these examples in training when we introduce stress into a scenario. Sometimes an officer's commands to a suspect are unclear. They may be overly loud or confusing, or there may be no command at all if the officer is hyper-focused on the event. The offender who is not complying with an officer may not clearly understand or hear what the officer is saying, or even worse, the officer could be giving conflicting demands. Any of these can result in severe and tragic consequences for either the officer or the subject. These are stress- or fear-induced responses to highly emotional events. An officer who is experiencing unmanaged fear from the danger of not being able to determine what is in a subject's hands can have tragic results.

That is an example of how fear becomes a factor in police-citizen contacts. The example is a straightforward one. What happens if we introduce additional factors such as the subject matching the description of an armed robbery suspect? This will likely increase the fear in the officer. Seeing a gun obviously can produce heightened anxiety or fear in an officer. Watch and listen to a video from an officer's body-worn camera or dashcam when he finds a gun. Pay attention to the officer's voice when he first sees the gun. The officer will likely shout, "Gun!" to alert other officers. Listen carefully to the voice inflection, and you will likely hear components of the fear response.

What about the factors that the police do not know about? How do unknown factors affect an officer's fear and, more importantly, the officer's response to it? Are prejudices and biases another component of the fear response? Can ethnicity, skin color, and manner of dress affect our fear response? What about other environmental factors such as crime and poverty? Can they affect our fears? The answer is yes. All of these factors can contribute to the production of fear in us.

Some of the things that produce fear would seem irrational if we watched a video of them sitting in the comfort of our homes. We are not fearful watching the event because we are not in the event. We do not experience fear symptoms watching news coverage of a knife-wielding subject the police are trying to talk to because we are not in that environment.

Watch the dashcam video of Van Dyke shooting McDonald, and it is likely that it will not produce heightened anxiety. We have nothing to fear from the subject because we are not there, and the brain knows it. We can watch those scenarios and come to rational conclusions about what the police could have done to be safe and de-escalate the situation. We can see the distances, available cover, and physical barriers that could protect us from the attack. We naturally reason about what is occurring as we watch it. However, this reasoning is not a part of the reality because we are not there and are not managing our fear at the same time.

The police do not get to experience these events in a safe and protected environment. The police experience them in real time on the street where the brain does not have the luxury of assuring them that an event is not dangerous. The brain is trying to sort things out in the presence of fear symptoms that, if not managed effectively, can easily confuse us. On the street, things happen very quickly, and as marvelous as the brain is, it is working hard to make sense out of these tense, uncertain, and rapidly evolving events.

Shooting at a moving vehicle is an excellent scenario to examine rational thinking in a use-of-force event. Few people would consider shooting at a moving vehicle to be a rational solution to stopping a car. A handgun bullet has little probability of stopping a large object like a car. However, we see it all of the time. There is an exciting scene in the movie *Patton*[36] during which George C. Scott's character, Patton, uses a handgun to shoot at a German airplane attacking a town. There is little chance that Patton is going to have any success in shooting down that airplane. Most of us would immediately recognize the futility of what Patton was doing and conclude that it was irrational. Was Patton reacting to fear symptoms by shooting at the airplane? We know it is unlikely Patton was ever afraid, right? Alternatively, were the other officers who remained in the office under a desk the ones that were reacting to fear by fleeing from it? The answer is, "It depends."

Putting General Patton's exploits aside, let us take a look at the dynamics of shooting at a moving vehicle. Let us assume that the facts support the reasonableness of the officer firing at the vehicle. Often the officer will explain that he was shooting at the driver, not the car. It is debatable how effective that actually can be, but it does happen. We know that rarely does a single bullet, or even multiple ones, stop an individual immediately. However, if it did, you now have a vehicle that will continue to travel until it crashes into something. There will be collateral damage from that car that we cannot predict. Our officers receive firearms training that teaches them to identify their targets and know what else could be impacted by a bullet they fire. If the officer is successful shooting at the motor vehicle and disabling the driver, where is that out of control car going? What is it going to hit? We have no way of knowing. Most of us, watching a movie in our living rooms, would say it is an irrational act with little likelihood of success. Yet on the street, we still do it. Why do we do it? The answer may lie, at least in part, in our fear responses.

The science[37] tells us there are many factors beyond our rational awareness that affect us when we are involved in a high-stress event, which can all combine to produce an officer's survival reaction. A vehicle moving in the direction of the officer may become the only thing the officer sees. The officer may experience time, distance, and spatial orientation distortions. The speed of the vehicle may appear faster or slower but, in any event, different than the reality that it is. The vehicle may not be traveling toward the officer at all, but at that moment, the officer is sure that it is.

Moreover, the vehicle may appear very large in the officer's vision and closer than it is. It can appear larger than it is to the point that it fills all of the officer's field of vision, making it more significant than it is. The officer only sees the vehicle as a threat and reacts to it by shooting at it, jumping out of the way, or in some cases being struck by it. Things are happening very quickly. The brain is processing a tremendous amount of information, and the officer acts or does not. Similar responses can occur during a subject encounter if the subject approaches the officer rapidly and is in an excited state.

These examples are genuine and happen routinely across our country. We do not teach officers to shoot at moving vehicles. Many police use-of-force policies specifically prohibit shooting at a moving vehicle when the vehicle is the only threat. Accordingly, if the vehicle is the only weapon and the officer does not have a reason to believe the occupants are armed, the officer should not shoot the car. We also teach officers not to reach into cars, but we see it happen often. This can result in an officer-involved shooting, and even though the initial reach in the car is discouraged, most of these shootings are deemed to be reasonable. They are considered reasonable because the driver is attempting to evade arrest and is presenting a threat that could reasonably produce serious bodily injury or death to the officer and bystanders. We may not like these scenarios, but they are often considered reasonable.

If we accept for a moment that a use of force was initially reasonable, why does it become excessive? Why were multiple baton strikes delivered to a subject who does not appear to be resisting? Why do the police continue to fire multiple rounds at a subject who has been struck by a bullet and is immobilized? Why did that initial reasonableness become unreasonable and excessive? It may be the result of an energy release. This energy release can be uncontrolled, irrational, and thus unreasonable because the rational decision-making process is not guiding the response; the fear response is.

The officer may not acknowledge the fear or may not even know that it is there, but most likely, it is. In a training environment, officers who use force are expected to justify their actions. Many explain that they were in fear. Often this is merely a learned answer to the instructor to justify their use of force. We have gotten away from allowing that and no longer accept that basic answer to a complex set of circumstances. Now we require students to explain their actions and include the facts presented to them and their force response to those facts. A thought-provoking point here is that the fear response may be the most accurate answer.

Rational thinking will eventually dominate the fear-driven response and ultimately control the officer's actions, and the baton strikes or trigger pulls will cease. However, what can occur between an officer's initial reaction to the stimuli and that rational decision-making ability to gain control is what can cause the problem. How many baton strikes or trigger pulls occurred between that initial release of prehistoric man's survival energy and the rational decision to stop because the threat has ceased to exist? Unfortunately, we know it can be significant.

Reaction time is the interval from the time we see something until we take action on it. For an example of reaction time, let us examine a driving scenario. Two cars are traveling an average speed of fifty miles per hour. The driver of the first car applies the brakes, and the brake lights illuminate. The driver of the second car sees those illuminated brake lights and applies the brakes on his vehicle as well. Reaction time is the time between when that second driver saw the illuminated brake lights and physically applied the brakes. The reaction time for most of us is generally about three-quarters of a second, but as we age, it begins to increase. That means that once we see the brake lights, it takes most of us three-quarters of a second to recognize we may need to apply the brakes and move our feet from the accelerator the short distance to the brake pedal and depress it. Distance interval recommendations between cars consider this reaction time by drivers. The average person has this limited understanding of reaction time, but there is another reaction time equation: the time needed to stop doing something. An officer needs to be concerned about both the time needed to react to an event and the time needed to stop reacting to that same event.

We started teaching this use-of-force reaction science thanks to the great work of Dr. Bill Lewinski at the Force Science Institute.[38] Essentially, the research revealed that there is an amount of time between when an officer perceives a threat and reacts to it. There is also the amount of time between when the officer recognizes that the threat ceased to exist and the need to react to the cessation and stop using force. Before the officer's actions, and during them, the subject is doing things as well. Some believe that this theory is misinformation designed to manipulate the facts to exonerate officers from instances of excessive use of force. Others believe it reflects the actual science of a use-of-force event and neither exonerates nor justifies an officer's actions.

While I was working in southwestern Pennsylvania, the USEPA agreed to do a scientific study of the impact of hydraulic fracturing on groundwater. Proponents of the study believed that science would be a reliable indicator of what was occurring. Passions, emotions, and opinions may have produced strong beliefs, but it would be the science that gave us the truth. Science exists in the absence of emotions, bias, or opinion. If that is the case, let us take an even closer look at the science surrounding police use of force.

The research is generally consistent on the amount of time it takes for a police officer to perceive something, determine it to be a threat, and react to it. Generally, across all officers, this reaction time is about three-quarters of a second to about a second and a half. In some cases, it can even be slower than that because a police officer is trained to consider many factors before pressing the trigger. These factors include target identification, which includes determining where it is; determining the certainty of it; determining the possible collateral damage that could occur; and determining the possible consequences that could result if the officer uses deadly force. A police officer may process all of that information before pressing the trigger. The average subject shooter does not.

Target identification and the time that it takes to shoot are critical when shooting skeet or sporting clays. As a veteran police officer and firearms instructor, I have consistently shot at the expert level with handguns, shotguns, and rifles. As a young boy, I recall pheasant and quail hunting and quickly taking down birds in full flight with a Winchester Model 12 shotgun. Not long ago, I received an invitation to participate in a day of shooting at a sporting clay facility, and I was really looking forward to it. Shooting at sporting clays was going to be fun, and I did not want to miss out on it. By the end of the day, I was embarrassed to be the worst shooter in the group. It did not seem possible, and it took me a while to figure it out. Critical to that kind of shooting is speed in reacting to the skeet or sporting clay and the ability to immediately fire. Without the speed, the target will quickly be out of range, and misses will occur more often than hits. My problem was target identification and analysis. I did not press the trigger until I was sure of my target. What was I being sure of? There was no other target. However, my forty-year law enforcement career taught me to first identify the target and then make a decision about whether or not to shoot. The target kept moving away from me and was out of range by the time I concluded my analysis and shot at it. I was behind the reactionary curve, and I shot slower than my teammates, none of whom were law enforcement officers.

The Force Science research also gave us time intervals when repeatedly pressing the trigger and firing a round. We call this time a rate of fire. Generally speaking, a handgun will fire as fast as the shooter can press the trigger, but exactly how fast is that? This time is generally consistent among both the average police officer and the average person. Recall for a moment that we are not training police officers to be competitive shooters, so their general fire rates are the same as everyone else with one caveat—target identification. Police officers cannot just keep pressing the trigger. They are responsible for every round they fire so, when firing, an officer needs to be concerned about collateral damage and must cease firing when the threat no longer exists. The bad guy, on the other hand, is not concerned about collateral damage or the shooting of uninvolved people.

Considering all of these factors, the rate of fire for most people is about a quarter or .25 seconds. What exactly does that mean in the real world? It means that a shooter can fire five rounds in one second. Think about that for a moment. The first shot fired is number one, another one fired at a quarter of a second is number two, a third fired at one-half second, a fourth at three-quarters of a second, and a fifth at one second for a total of five rounds in one second.

This rate of fire is what we often find troubling in an unreasonable officer-involved-shooting. We are not surprised to see numerous rounds fired in a short amount of time in a high-stress event because, as described above, anyone can fire five rounds in one second. We are also not surprised when these rounds do not strike the intended target due to the higher rates of fire that can be typical of an officer operating under stress. High rates of fire are often less accurate than slower, more deliberate ones. However, it becomes troubling when we see multiple rounds fired accurately over a higher than expected amount of time. We rarely see this scenario, but when we do, it often does not work out well for the officer.

Another study looked at how long it takes for officers to decide to stop shooting after they started. This time was also generally from about three-quarters of a second to a second and a half. Using these results, you can conclude that if an officer takes a second and a half to stop shooting in a tense, uncertain, and rapidly evolving deadly force event, that officer could easily fire six, seven, eight, or more rounds after he decides to stop shooting. This is not much time and demonstrates the possible reactions to a highly stressful, deadly force situation. As I wrote earlier, things happen very quickly on the street. Since the officer can quickly fire several rounds as soon as he begins to shoot, you can see how the total number of rounds can be significant. In a matter of just a few seconds, an officer could easily fire numerous rounds, which, to the untrained, can appear excessive. However, when we examine the various time factors in play, the facts tell us otherwise. Fact-based science tells us that an officer could easily fire a high number of rounds in a short period.

Readers might be thinking that these numbers are misleading and are offered in an effort to exonerate the many rounds fired by the police. Oftentimes, we do not want to believe or accept what we do not like. Some may not like the science or accept it because of the anger they have for the police. The anger is understandable, but the science stands.

We know many factors influence action and reaction times, and those times can be slightly longer or shorter. We also know that it takes time for an officer to act on a perceived threat and to stop those actions. During all of this time, other things are happening. Consider a police-involved shooting. A subject is generally facing toward the officer when encountered. He produces what the officer believes to be a gun, points it at the officer, and then turns to run away. If the officer decides to fire, at least some of the rounds fired may strike the subject in the back. The Force Science research shows us the same results time and again regardless of the ages of subjects and officers. An officer's reactions to a subject's actions take time. The officer will be firing on what was, and the result will not match what is. The officer could fire one or more rounds before consciously seeing the turned subject, resulting in rounds entering the subject in the rear. Officers often tell us that when they fired the subject was facing them, and yet the subject was shot in the back. The officer's assertions and the physical evidence showing the bullet's entry can both be true because it takes time for an officer to react to a suspect's actions, and it takes time to fire those rounds.

Use-of-force events, and specifically officer-involved shootings, take time. They take time to start, they continue for some time, and they take time to stop. While time is elapsing, many things are happening. The suspect is doing things, the officer is processing information, the officer is acting, and environmental factors may be occurring. Time does not stop these factors from occurring. Time continues to move on. As I wrote elsewhere in this book, there are no unimportant facts in a police use-of-force event, and this is the reason.

Some people do not want to believe this science, and it can be even less believable when the subject is later found to have been unarmed, or the subject is a person of color, and the cop is white. Some people will believe that the police officer intentionally shot the unarmed person in the back while he was running away. I do not know a single officer who thought it was reasonable for former North Charleston Officer Michael Slager to shoot Walter Scott.[39] However, all police officers who shoot an unarmed person, even in the back, are not criminals. Some of them reacted to the events presented to them with tragic results. We need to separate our judgment of officer-involved shootings we do not like from those that are unreasonable.

Body-worn and vehicle dash-mounted cameras are widely used by most law enforcement agencies today. They are useful because they give us a view of a situation that we would not have had. In *Scott v. Harris,* the Court took time to view the recordings of the police vehicle's dashboard camera. While these videos are relevant evidence, consider what we see in the videos. We see what the camera saw, not necessarily what the officer was seeing. Unless we wire cops to monitor heart rate, blood pressure, and brain function, the video alone does not tell the whole story. Recall the many physiological factors that affect sensory preceptors during a high-stress event. Akin to a confession, a video does not stand alone. Albeit important, it is merely one piece of evidence in a comprehensive investigation.

In addition to fight-or-flight responses, there is also the freeze response. This is the one that most concerns police trainers because it creates danger for the officer and fellow officers. The officer's inability to act results in indecision, and the officer does nothing. The freeze response is characterized by an inability of the officer to flee for safety or to fight the threat. The officer does nothing and becomes either a casualty or an embarrassment in his mind. Trainers often see this response in room-entry drills. An officer or two are told to enter a room and watch for subjects that may be a threat to them. Many times, the officer enters the doorway and neither enters the room nor backs out of it. He remains in the doorway. We teach officers that the doorway is the most dangerous place to be. This "fatal funnel" creates a choke point that makes officers highly vulnerable to an attack, but they still do it. Fear of the unknown in the room, fear of making a mistake in front of the instructor, or some other fear results in the officer freezing. Freezing or the inability to act is an unmanaged fear response. Officers can freeze in training, or worse, they can freeze on the streets.

We all experience fear in some way, and police officers are no different from anyone else. That fear may be of something as minimal as a written test in school or as dangerous as confronting a violent, armed offender. We know what makes fear difficult to manage is not so much the fear but the symptoms the fear produces. If we allow our sympathetic bodily systems that respond to fear to proceed unmanaged, it is difficult for us to reason. We are subconsciously more concerned about staying alive than we are about rational thinking. A citizen might be able to get away with these unchecked systems, but a police officer cannot. For instance, a citizen in a bar fight may not need to be concerned with extra strikes, punches, or kicks. The police officer, on the other hand, must be reasonable and cannot allow his survival instincts to control him. The police officer needs to stop when it is no longer reasonable to exert the level of force he is using. That means shutting down those survival systems and rationally thinking about what to do next. It can be challenging to take a 160, 180, or even higher beats per minute heart rate down to a manageable 120 beats per minute. Also challenging is switching from the narrow vision he has been hyper-focused on (the threat) to the wider surrounding area and transitioning from rapid, short breaths to slower, beneficial breaths.

How do we teach our officers to control fear systems so they can make rational decisions? We work on the ability to apply some amount of rational control on the effect that fear has on them. We know that officers who experience something in training can later respond to a similar event in an improved way. We know that officers who have more knowledge about what they are doing are more comfortable and can manage fear more effectively. They can experience a highly stressful event and not allow the survival systems to control their actions. Instead, they can readily exert rational control over what is happening.

During firearms training, we conduct a drill designed to help normalize body systems. We teach officers to focus on a target threat and, if and when appropriate, to fire at it to stop it. If we successfully present the training, the officer's bodily systems are in full survival mode, and we want them to control those reactions and rationally think about what else they need to do. It is called looking for work in tactics. We teach officers to turn their heads to the left and right and look to the rear and to verbalize something like "suspect down" or "clear," and we teach them to breathe. One of the primary reasons for this drill is to teach awareness. Officers are taught to determine if there are other threats (to the sides and rear) and to communicate with other officers. The other, often overlooked, benefit to this drill is the shock we deliver to the body's survival systems and expediting their return to normalcy. Moving the focus off of the threat, verbalization, and breathing all help the body get out of the survival mode and return it to the thinking mode. This allows the officer to attend to other necessary tasks.

Some use-of-force instructors teach the mantra, "Threat, weapon, area." I teach officers to first make sure they control the threat or "effectively neutralize" the threat. Next, officers need to check the condition of their firearm if they fired rounds to neutralize the threat. Is the weapon functional, or does something need to be corrected? Do you still have ammunition, or do you need to reload? What about the area? Is there anything else in the area that is concerning such as additional suspects, bystanders, or officers?

A use-of-force training that I recently participated in is an excellent example of the importance of understanding situational awareness. In one particular scenario, it was necessary for me to use deadly force to stop an armed suspect. The instructor conducting the exercise kept repeating the words, "Threat, weapon, area," because he saw something that I did not. I was so focused on the threat and radioing information about the shooting that I failed to notice that my handgun was not functional. The slide locked to the rear, rendering it incapable of being fired. The shooting was reasonable, but I failed to regain rational thought quickly, and in doing so, I placed myself and others in a dangerous situation. It happens in training, and it happens on the street.

All of this may sound simple while reading words in a book. However, on the street, things are a lot different. All the things I wrote about become factors that are not in a controlled, training environment but are amid the uncontrolled chaos on the street. The street can be a dangerous place with very violent occurrences. You do not have to ask a cop. Ask the people who live in these communities.

Even the best-trained officers can act unreasonably in a given situation. People react differently to different stimuli at different times. It is complicated. Sometimes the police did everything they reasonably could have, and someone still was severely injured or died. Sometimes these people were unarmed. The death of a subject or the death of a police officer is never the result we want. The wise words of a police officer, "Everyone goes home alive," should always be the goal.

Most police actions across this country are reasonable. We do not always like them, but they are. When they are not, they need to be acknowledged and corrected. Some officers are fired, and some go to jail, but most of the time, we learn from mistakes, improve the police, and can expect better results. People generally improve when presented with a better way of doing things. The police are the people too.

CHAPTER FOUR
THE CYNIC

Ever wonder where cynicism in policing comes from or why officers become cynical? Look no further than some of the people they come in contact with every day.

Chapter 4
The Cynic

A cop does not work at being cynical. It is not a merit badge. It just happens. If it was learned behavior, then maybe it could be unlearned, but it is not. Cynicism is another one of those insidious invasions of a police officer's mind, body, and spirit. It starts with the pride of wearing the uniform. It starts with looking in the mirror the first time that uniform is worn for real and the pride that comes with wearing it. The uniform is the result of the hard work it took to earn the right to wear it. People on the street are going to see that pride as well. The good people are glad to see a cop, and the bad guys are not. That command presence wields an incredible amount of authority. "I am finally a cop," and that means just about everything at that moment.

Unfortunately, that moment does not last very long, and working the street becomes a new reality. That new uniform becomes soiled, stained, and torn. Everyone is not excited to see the young officer, and they do not always cooperate. Most of the people the officer comes in contact with have a story that is somewhere between truth and fiction.

The first lie was told to me by a United States Air Force (USAF) recruiter. I enlisted in the air force to become a security policeman. In other words, a military policeman who did all of the things civilian cops did. The recruiter was glad to oblige, but the reason he was so eager only became apparent much later.

At that time, the air force designated its law enforcement personnel "security police" rather than the more common term "military police" used in other branches. Since that time, Security Police have been redesignated and are now the "United States Air Force Security Forces," which probably more accurately reflects their primary mission. The 812XX career field was what we would recognize as the base police or military police in other branches. The 811XX career field, however, comprised the only combat-trained unit in the USAF, and they were responsible for defending the air base. The XXs were numeric and reflected one's level of competency in the given career field. The 811s were responsible for air base ground defense, the security of aircraft and missiles, and all of the nuclear weapons in the USAF inventory.

In 1973, the USAF had plenty of nuclear weapons loaded on airplanes, sitting atop missiles in silos, and stored in weapon storage areas in both the continental United States and overseas. The USAF, through its Strategic Air Command, was responsible for two prongs of America's nuclear triad defense system: missiles and aircraft. The other, of course, was the United States Navy's ballistic submarines. The high number of security police personnel needed for nuclear weapons security left air force recruiters with constant challenges to meet enlistment quotas in the 811XX career field. Recruiters had few 812XX slots but were always in need of 811XX enlistees.

I was an 811XX, with all the rights and privileges that came with it. It took a while for the reality of this deception to register with me. It became clear on a cold night in January 1974, while I was standing at the nose of a B-52 bomber as it was being uploaded with nuclear weapons on the ramp at Minot Air Force Base in North Dakota. The sixty below zero chill factor wind that night seemed to clarify things.

The second lie the recruiter told me was about the base of choice dream sheet that turned out to be just that, a dream. On second thought, maybe he did not lie after all. I was a security policeman with a badge and gun, and I got to dream of the Homestead and McGuire Air Force bases that were on the base selection lists. I guess it depends on how you look at it.

I am not the first person to be lied to by a military recruiter, and I certainly will not be the last. Military recruiters have been perfecting that magical craft since General George Washington crossed the Delaware River. Lou Manfredo's character, NYPD Detective Sergeant Joe Rizzo said, "There is no wrong, there is no right, there just is."[40]

I do not know the first time someone lied to me on the street, but I remember one of the worst ones. It resulted in only a verbal reprimand, but it could have been a lot more serious. I gave a guy a break, trusting he would surrender himself on a warrant as he said he would. He did not, and I looked foolish. Worse than that was the nonfeasance, essentially not doing the job that I was sworn to do pursuant to a court order. I should have arrested him on the spot. Fortunately, I had a sergeant who understood leadership and used my screwup as an opportunity to learn what I already thought I knew.

I would hear many more lies throughout my police career. Often it was because I was trying to give someone a break or a chance to make things right. However, no one who ever had an outstanding arrest warrant ever got a break from me again. From then on, when someone pleaded with me to avoid arrest, I responded with the command, "Place your hands behind your back," and I applied handcuffs. I wonder if I became just a little bit more cynical about trusting people after that day. The sad part is that there were probably many people who went to jail because they could not afford a couple of hundred dollars. They might have done the right thing if given a chance.

Oh well, I started to learn the lessons that members of the public were teaching. I learned only to trust what my partner or I verified.

Everything else was suspect. Cynicism develops slowly and feeds on multiple aspects of an officer's professional and personal life. It develops synergy from a combination of factors, each of which on their own would appear to be insignificant. Together though, they create the prism of cynicism through which the officer sees the world.

Consider the roll answering calls for service plays into feeding an officer's cynical views. Most police departments today use a computer-aided dispatch (CAD) system. The CAD helps prioritize calls so that high-priority ones receive a timely police response, particularly when lives are at stake. The lower-priority calls can wait. People figured this out though, and although their need for the police may not be a high priority in the grander scheme, it is to them. They want a cop at their problem immediately. So people learned that the word *gun* will usually get them an immediate police response. The call about a suspicious-looking male standing on the corner may not get much of a response. Make that same call and say the suspicious male looks like he has a gun—and now you get an immediate police response.

The manager of the local convenience store wants the shoplifter apprehended, but the police are too slow. The manager figures out that the shoplifter who may have a gun will get the cops there right away. So now you have officers all converging on the store with guns drawn for a shoplifter because the manager wanted the cops there quickly. As a result, the cops risk their lives with a hot response to a man with a gun call which is, in reality, a low-priority call. They confront an unarmed shoplifter with guns drawn, and their anxiety is high. That is a recipe for disaster if the subject's hands are not visible, he does not comply, or he fails to understand police instructions, makes perceived threatening movements, or has something in his hand that could be a weapon. Ever wonder why the police shot an unarmed shoplifter? That is an example.

The other thing that can happen is the "man with a gun" shoplifter call happens too many times. Then one day there is a real "man with a gun" call which is both a danger to the citizenry and the cops because it is assumed to be another false call. How many times does the false call have to happen before the cynic cop thinks that the "man with a gun" call is probably just another attempt to get the police there sooner? Ever wonder where cynicism in policing comes from or why officers become cynical? Look no further than some of the people they come in contact with every day.

I learned about United States Code Title 18 Section 1001, in the Criminal Investigator Training Program, which is basic training for federal agents. The law essentially says that lying to a federal agent is a crime. False statements have been in the news a lot lately and are associated with the various federal investigations surrounding the 2016 presidential election. The FBI arrested several people for lying. The news media claims that lying to the FBI is a federal crime. That is true, but the statute applies to any federal law enforcement officer and not just the FBI. Over my long federal career, I saw that charge many times in an indictment, a plea, or a conviction. Currently, subjects are being arrested and charged with false statements or lying in connection with the federal election fraud investigation. These charges would be comical if they were not so sad because many people lie, and every cop out there sees it every day.

Cops expect people to lie, end of story. The driver of a car stopped for speeding is going to lie. The motorist will say he did not know how fast he was going or did not realize he was speeding. It is rare that a driver admits to speeding. If he tells the truth, he may even get a break from the officer because his candor will be a surprise. A burglary suspect, when asked about other crimes, will say this was his first. A victim of domestic violence may deny being assaulted when asked, despite the apparent injuries.

Cops learn early in their careers that everyone lies, and they begin to accept it as a way of life. If there is a learned behavior, it is that some cops lie, particularly when they get jammed up and are the subject of an internal investigation. Federally, more special agents lose their careers for lack of candor than for any other offense. They have learned to lie from the public they dealt with most of their career.

Cynicism sounds like something bad or at least an undesirable trait to have. A little bit of cynicism, however, can be useful. Cynicism tells us that the link embedded in an email from a friend is probably fraudulent and will not lead to free money. Not being cynical about the email and accepting it for face value may cause serious computer problems. "There is no such thing as a free lunch" might be another cynical observation.

To the police officer, good cynical traits are those that keep her safe and out of trouble. If it does not sound right and does not feel right, then there is a good chance that it is not. If a cop thinks there is an ulterior motive, there very well may be. Those free NFL tickets that the local tavern owner wants to give the cop who patrols his street may not be just because the owner likes cops. The free meal or discounted meal at a local diner may come with ulterior motives. The cynical officer believes nothing is free. The owner is going to want something someday. Something that she may not want to do or legally cannot do. It may or may not be true, but the cynical officer goes with the probability that it is. The officer avoids doing something wrong because she knows it is likely to resurface unpleasantly. A certain amount of cynicism in cops is a good thing. It keeps them safe.

The cynicism that is problematic is cynicism coupled with bias. It can take root early in a police officer's career and can become a very ugly and pervasive character trait. The idea and belief that everyone lies to the police is accepted early, so we are cynical that it will always be that way. But what about "Everyone on that block is a drug dealer"? While it may be true that there are many drug dealers on the block, it is likely that not all residents on that block deal drugs.

Cynicism coupled with bias is a slippery slope on which some officers begin to slide. The mistrust that becomes a part of who we are is complicated by the implicit bias that is present in all of us. We all have opinions and likes and dislikes about different things. Very few of us have no opinion about anything, although I have known a few cops who got to that point. Even in those extreme cases, those cops still demonstrate strong opinions about policing. In their world, there are cops, and there is everybody else. Cynicism fuels bias, and the synergy is usually both strong and dangerous. It creates a recipe for bad things to happen.

Most cops do not have a conscious bias against anyone for the color of their skin, religion, dress, hairstyle, or any other reason. That does not sound believable, but it is true. If we can agree that we as a people have implicit biases, then we can include cops since we are people too. Police cynicism evolves from a career of seeing people doing bad things, not so much from bias.

Cops see the worst humanity has to offer. Skin color, religion, dress, or hairstyle are not prerequisites for people to do bad things. Cops see white, brown, and black professionals who commit acts of deliberate violence such as beating their spouses, using illegal drugs, and engaging with prostitutes. It does not stop there; it continues with the corruption that robs people of their savings and destroys trust in financial institutions. Cops also see white, brown, and black people who live in poverty and commit crimes of violence, including robberies and narcotics trafficking. Whatever bias the police officer brings to the event is overshadowed by the developed cynicism that suggests that all people are capable of anything.

At the beginning of this chapter, I indicated that cynicism could not be unlearned because it is not learned. Cynicism insidiously invades our beings and becomes a part of who we are as cops. Remember everybody lies, and we cannot trust anyone. That sounds harsh, but it is the evolution that occurs in the mind of a police officer. The fundamental reason that it cannot be unlearned is that the officer finds little, if anything, to suggest that it is not true. Street experiences continuously reinforce the officer's cynicism. In some busy patrol areas, it happens every single day. It becomes a way of life for the officer.

Sometimes cynicism, at its worst, comes from the people the police are trying to help. Most of the violence in America today is alarming. Almost every day, and often several times a day, we hear about gun violence. We then hear pleas from police and public officials for the public to come forward to help solve these crimes. In areas where the police have a good relationship with the public, people cooperate. In other places, the mistrust runs deep, witnesses remain silent, and violent offenders remain on the street to prey upon other victims.

The police are cynical about receiving help from the public, and the public does not trust the police enough to cooperate with them. Cynicism needs to be reality tested. It survives and grows in the absence of reality. We believe things are the way they are, and if there is little evidence that they can be different, we will remain cynical. The cynicism that nothing is going to improve, everyone lies, and no one can be trusted continues on both sides.

Active community engagement can sow the seeds of change. It can begin to build trust in both the police and the public by revealing the reality of what is. Cynicism may not disappear in either group, but the effects of community engagement can begin to shift the negative to positive. If we can agree that the people are the police and the police are the people, then we should be able to understand how cynicism can exist because it can exist in all of us.

More importantly, what can we do about it? If we can understand how to minimize it in ourselves, then maybe we can accept that it can be minimized in others as well. The alternative is to continue on the path we are on. Cynicism runs deep, and it is not working.

CHAPTER FIVE

THE EXPENDABLES IN AMERICA

This woman's husband fought bravely in Korea for his country, the United States of America. She, however, did not have clean water to drink.

Chapter 5
The Expendables in America

If this is a book about policing, what does this chapter have to do with it? To some, the word *police* itself has morphed into something unrecognizable from its original definition. My first years as a policeman were more simply defined. The police were the police, and that was it. However, lives were more simply defined then too. Life is much more complicated now and so are the complexities of policing.

In the police academy, I learned that criminal law derived from the common law of the land. Criminal law started out as rights and wrongs as society saw them. Historically, they were the norms and were easily recognizable to most people. The model penal code, which is the basis of most criminal law today, is much more complicated, and the rights and wrongs are not as easy to understand. Not that long ago, highly technological computer crimes did not exist. Complex frauds were merely larcenies, and there were no government regulations that, although civil in their intent to regulate, also contained criminal provisions.

The law enforcement terminology of today is much broader and captures the broader responsibilities of law and order. Federal agents, criminal investigators, and even prosecutors are law enforcement and by association become the police. Take a look at the printing on the back of a federal agent's raid jacket. It is a safe bet that the word "police" will be there somewhere. I learned over the years that my opinion that the police and law enforcement were distinctly different, or at least not the same thing, was generally wrong. Law enforcement is appropriate terminology and encompasses the wide-ranging responsibilities vested upon it by the people of the United States of America.

I am a member of the International Association of Chiefs of Police and serve as a member of the Environmental Crimes Committee. Environmental crimes encompass a highly specialized area of law enforcement that is similar in many ways to complex frauds. Most prosecutable environmental crimes involve lying, cheating, and stealing. Early in my career, our police department became involved in these investigations because we were in a rural area that was attractive to criminals looking for a place to dump debris and chemicals that resulted in environmental pollution.

I had no interest in environmental crimes. My background up until that point was patrol and highway safety. In other words, all in uniform. However, we were forming a new state police-funded unit called Emergency Management, and with the promise of sergeant's stripes at some point, the chief convinced me to accept the assignment of operations officer. In addition to the emergency management function, the unit was also responsible for investigating environmental crimes.

One of the early investigations involved the theft and burning of copper wire. A few men trying to generate income from scrap metal obtained large amounts of copper wire, some of it stolen, and burnt the insulation off of it in large open fires. The burning would usually occur late at night, and sometimes the intense smoke would travel into residential areas, creating a dangerous situation for the people living there. On one particular night, a firefighter became overcome by the smoke, and the area needed to be evacuated. The public wanted action, and the chief instructed me to do something about it. I did what any cop would do. One night, I locked up everybody at the fire scene and towed their vehicles.

With the assistance of criminal investigators from the New Jersey Attorney Generals' Environmental Crimes Unit, I charged everyone with several environmental crimes. As a result, the fires stopped, and people no longer had to tolerate the smoke in their neighborhoods. The prosecutor, however, declined prosecution because we had not met the elements of the crime charged. Specifically, the prosecutor said that there was no intent to commit an environmental crime. All of the subjects pled guilty to an amended disorderly persons offense. Today, all of the sites where the burnings occurred have been deemed dioxin-contaminated hazardous waste sites.

Although we did not have a successful criminal prosecution, we were satisfied with the outcome because we helped the people of that community. That outcome is very similar to much of what I write about in this chapter, and it all relates to people. The impact on the people is what forced us to act, and people are at the core of everything the police do. If anyone is wondering, the answer is yes. I did get stripes a couple of years later.

In my experience, there are few prosecutable environmental crimes. The anecdote I use is that law enforcement investigates less than 10 percent of the total number of environmental violations or offenses known. We criminally prosecute less than 1 percent of the 10 percent we investigate. Most environmental issues are appropriately dealt with by regulatory entities such as federal or state environmental protection agencies. However, all of these events (accidents, regulatory violations, intentional acts, or crimes) involve people. Pollution exposes, impacts, and forces people to live in affected areas. These incidents are less about the environment and more about people, and policing is about people.

Policing is much less about cops and robbers and locking up bad guys than it is about solving people's problems. Policing is about people, the negative things they are experiencing, and the role police have in curtailing those experiences. One cop I know recently said that he changed more flat tires than the number of people he arrested. Cops are reading this and know that even the lockups they make travel a circuitous route through the criminal justice system. Seldom are they called to testify at a criminal trial as the result of an arrest. Most arrests result in pretrial interventions, plea bargains, drug courts, or remands to a lower court. Few work their way through the criminal justice system to trial. If we can accept that policing is about people, that it is not about enforcing laws enacted under the evolution of technology and regulations, then maybe what I write about in this chapter will make a little more sense. Maybe the blameless victimization of people is consistent with what a cop sees across geographical, political, social, and racial lines. I saw a lot of expendable people in my career. This was just a different variation of the same old thing.

The current New Jersey attorney general (AG), Gurbir Grewal, recently announced an initiative targeting the victimization of polluted minority communities. The AG cited numerous instances where minority communities have become dumping grounds for corporate polluters. These are the communities where we built our wastewater treatment plants with all of their noxious odors. The factories that once produced important staples for our economy are now abandoned, leaving behind contamination. The AG, in a very public press conference, announced a task force to correct the wrongs in these expendable communities. *Expendable* is a strong word to use, but I have seen firsthand the victimization of the people who live in these communities, and I do not know what else to call it.

For more than fifteen years, I was a United States special agent employed by the Environmental Protection Agency's Criminal Investigation Division (USEPA-CID). Most people do not know that many agencies within the federal government employ criminal investigators. These agencies—including Housing and Urban Development, Department of the Interior, and the Environmental Protection Agency—employ United States special agents to investigate criminal acts within their area of responsibility. Some of these special agents, like at EPA, have full law enforcement authority to enforce any federal law—even if their duties do not routinely call upon them to do it. These special agents may carry firearms and make arrests for federal felonies anywhere in the United States or its territories. So, for example, an EPA special agent can arrest a bank robber or a hijacker on a commercial aircraft. Some states also designate federal agents from identify specific agencies as law enforcement officers in their respective states. Most states, for instance, will recognize the special agents of the Federal Bureau of Investigation (FBI), Alcohol Tobacco and Firearms (ATF), and the Drug Enforcement Agency (DEA) as state law enforcement officers.

During my service as a special agent, I was at one point stationed at USEPA-CID's Philadelphia Area Office. The Philadelphia Area Office's area of responsibility included Delaware, Maryland, Virginia, Pennsylvania, West Virginia, and the District of Columbia. The entire state of Pennsylvania was worked out of the Philadelphia office even though our Wheeling, West Virginia, office was closer to many areas of Pennsylvania. The West Virginia, Ohio, and New York offices were much closer to many areas of Pennsylvania, but the geopolitical lines did not permit special agents assigned to those offices to work Pennsylvania cases. As absurd as that sounds, we had no other office in the entire state of Pennsylvania. It made no sense because it created a hindrance on a criminal investigator's need to develop information sources and coordinate with other law enforcement officers in the area. The responsibility for that decision rested squarely on the EPA, a civil agency, and not the criminal investigation division of that agency. It is my understanding that some of that guidance has changed, as it should.

One of my first trips to western Pennsylvania was to monitor an EPA public meeting about natural gas drilling. The meeting, in Washington County, was one of several, and it was intended to allow people to voice their opinions about horizontal drilling and hydraulic fracturing. This relatively new process to Pennsylvania was occurring to extract the vast amount of natural gas found deep in the Marcellus shale. A wide range of gas drilling proponents and opponents attended the meeting, and they all had firm opinions about it.

During that meeting, I took note of some of the private citizens who spoke and were living in the areas where drilling was occurring. They related stories about the environmental and health effects they claimed to be experiencing and wanted the federal government, through the EPA, to investigate the practice. I spoke privately with a few of these people after the meeting. Some claimed that their well water was not usable and that domestic animals had died from drinking it. They shared stories about making numerous complaints to state regulatory officials, but they did not believe that anyone was taking their complaints seriously. We arranged for follow-up visits to speak with them further and view the associated areas. People called on a cop, and a cop was going to show up.

Around the same time as this meeting, there was an environmental catastrophe in southwestern Pennsylvania that got the attention of the environmental science community. A stream known as Dunkard Creek had been the victim of what environmental protection agencies were calling a total aquatic kill. Mostly, that meant that everything that lived in the water died. Dunkard Creek is in southwestern Pennsylvania near the West Virginia border. Many factors influenced the water quality in Dunkard Creek, including the water draining from nearby coal mining operations. Some of the mines were no longer operating, but the drainage continued. Some people also suspected that wastewater associated with natural gas drilling caused this event. The environmental scientists at USEPA, the Pennsylvania Department of Environmental Protection, and West Virginia University were all investigating possible causes. The Dunkard Creek event, together with the controversies about natural gas drilling, created a new and intense focus on that very rural area. The EPA formed a task force of many talented environmental scientists and investigators and created a tip line to elicit information from the public. I was the only criminal investigator assigned to that task force, and thus, I became more entrenched in both the issues and the people who lived there.

Southwestern Pennsylvania is similar to many of the rural areas of Ohio, West Virginia, or even New York State. Families lived in these areas for generations and mostly enabled their livelihoods from minerals, primarily coal, which was abundantly mined there for the past 150 years or so. America has been steadily moving away from using coal and has been relying more on natural gas. Poverty is high in these areas since the jobs come and go with the human resource needs of the energy industries. The use of illegal drugs has risen to epidemic proportions and with that came a general deterioration of people's quality of life. It is not everywhere, and it is not everyone, but it is pervasive.

To me, although the geography was different, there was not much difference between the people I saw there and those I saw in the cities of Camden, Newark, or Elizabeth, New Jersey. The beautiful, rolling forested hills and green pastures replaced the concrete and steel, but the people were the same. Some of them were poor—or at least not rich—but were thankful to have a job that helped them provide for their families. They were just trying to live their lives despite what was going on around them. They were raising children as they always had. They sent them to school to get an education with the hope that their children's lives would be better than their own. They were fans of the Pittsburgh Steelers, the Pirates, the Penguins, the Panthers, and the West Virginia Mountaineers. They stood for the national anthem at these games and saluted our flag.

There were also people who escaped urban life and relocated to these rural areas to live and raise their families in a quieter, more serene environment. Sometimes they succeeded, and sometimes they did not. The business of energy resource extraction will always be a part of areas like these because of the vast amounts of the resources present and the ever-evolving technology to recover it. The coal mines have been there for a long time, and this new gas drilling method was just beginning.

Some people felt they moved away from industry only to find themselves back in it. A Pennsylvania Department of Environmental Protection Inspector put it best. His view was that heavy industry had dropped into the middle of a quiet, rural area. I often thought about that, and it reinforced what I already knew. People there were not any different from people from other places in America. People were people.

Heavy industry has always been a major employer of people, and often the employees lived in nearby neighborhoods. Most of the time, the factories were there first, attracted jobs, and communities sprung up around them. We can still see evidence of these communities in the neighborhoods of our cities where heavy industry once existed. Shipbuilding, chemical plants, and all sorts of manufacturing supported the communities that lived around them. That same kind of community development occurred in rural America around coal mines in the early 1900s.

During the Great Depression, my grandparents lived with their children in what was known as a coal company town in West Virginia. What started as small communities became hundreds of homes. They were more shacks than houses, but nevertheless were where the men who worked in the coal mines lived with their families. They were paid very little money and instead were compensated with company script. This script was used to pay the company for the rental of their house and to purchase needed staples from the company-owned stores. Little evidence of these towns exists today because as the mines closed, the towns were abandoned and either reclaimed by the land or razed.

Gas drilling, although similar to these examples, was different. Rather than communities developing around the drilling, the communities were already there, and the gas drilling sprung up among them. I saw well drilling in mobile home communities, in parks, and near schools. People said that the energy companies would drill anywhere the gas was. Gas drilling was also different than the mines because of the infrastructure needed to not only extract the gas but to move it to where it needed to go. Moving the gas requires compressor stations and an extensive pipeline system. Energy extraction technology came of age amid the people who already lived there.

I traveled out to southwestern Pennsylvania and the northern part of West Virginia numerous times over the next year. On one of my early trips out there, I quickly saw the passion in the people. My plan was to meet with one family, and about a dozen other families had also assembled in that home to talk to me. They coordinated and all wanted to talk to the federal agent who was going to help them. They all told a similar story, which I would hear over and over again in Washington County, Pennsylvania, Wetzell County, West Virginia, and numerous other places throughout these states. They suspected that their air and water had been contaminated by gas drilling. Although people complained to local congressional representatives, state regulatory officials, and the EPA, they maintained that no one was helping them with their problem. Most people in that area had private wells for drinking water. Many of them said that either their water or someone else's they knew was undrinkable because of color, taste, or odor. They told me about dead animals, sick kids, and a generally deteriorating way of life in the area where natural gas drilling was occurring. They talked about noxious odors in the air, which they claimed came from the hydraulic fracturing process necessary to develop gas wells. They also described the high heat and flames coming from the flaring of new wells that caused breathing difficulties for people in the immediate area.

The first time I saw a gas well flare was one evening while I was traveling on Interstate 79 near the Pennsylvania and West Virginia border. I saw a glow from the well, which was not too far off of the highway, and I almost immediately felt the heat. The heat was not like heat from a fire. It reminded me of the heat from an oven, similar to gas ovens in most houses, only greatly magnified. The other noticeable thing was the odor, which I cannot describe. The most significant thing was the lack of breathable air. It seemed that the oxygen level in the area must have been affected because it felt like I was having trouble getting my breath. It reminded me of a night surveillance I was working in a highly industrialized area of Northern New Jersey many years ago. Very early one morning, an odor permeated the entire area, and although there was no fire, I had a similar experience with a lack of breathable area. These experiences were very similar, and again were a testament that rural America is not that much different from our cities and the people who live there.

I left the Washington County meeting that night overwhelmed by what I heard. The meeting was very similar to other meetings I attended throughout my policing career: meetings with people living in high-crime areas who were victims of violence, drugs, and the general deterioration of their communities. It also reminded me of the pollution I witnessed in several New Jersey cities earlier in my career as a criminal investigator.

Southwestern Pennsylvania and West Virginia are not in the inner city. They are considered rural America. They are about clean air and beautiful landscapes. They are the places people go to escape the city. The geography may be different, but there was no difference in the people who lived there. Their way of life was being severely affected by things outside of their control. It is a matter of life and death to the people who live in these areas: death by bullets in an inner city full of violence and death by environmental factors in rural America. That may sound dramatic, and it is, except to the people who live there.

I did not know it then, but that trip was only the beginning. It would be the beginning of what so many cops experience as they become a part of the communities they police. They may not live there, but they become connected and immersed in the people and their problems. The cops care. They try to help, but they accomplish little and become just as frustrated as the people living there or even more so. It is not a good thing. It is not healthy, and it regularly happens to police officers across this country. My experience there is with me to this day.

I traveled to these rural areas many times to understand the nature and extent of what was occurring there. I met with dozens of people from the upper middle class to those in poverty, and the complaints were all similar. These people all believed they were being exposed to dangerous chemicals resulting from gas drilling, and they had plenty of stories and examples to support their claims.

Families claimed that kids were getting violently ill, and the medical professionals could not determine the causes. They talked about nausea and nosebleeds happening to small children. They told me that these were most prevalent when drilling activity occurred near their homes. I saw the orange-brown water in the toilets from the well-water servicing their homes. Because the well water was unusable, the people who could afford it had potable water delivered to their homes, and a few families were fortunate to have energy companies providing their water.

I met families who lived near wastewater impoundments generated by the gas well development in the area. They did not know what was causing their children to be ill or what caused their domestic animals to die. They just knew that it was happening. They pursued several avenues to investigate and solve these issues to no avail. State regulatory officials, representatives of the energy industries in the area, universities, and medical professionals were all unable to provide solutions. The medical professionals agreed the kids were sick and that it could be environmentally related, but their conclusions stopped there. The universities affirmed abnormal deaths of the domestic animals but did not conclude causation, only saying that they could be environmentally related. I listened to these stories, saw their dilemma, and felt their pain. I also knew that many of their issues would remain unsolved. These people were victims of circumstances beyond their control and were, in my opinion, expendable.

I have seen this same thing so many times in my career. People living in communities who are victimized by things outside of their control. What did this have to do with policing? The answer is in the title of this book—policing is about people. We want to solve problems, fix things, and make the world a better place. Sometimes it is just not possible. I saw it over and over again, and this was going to be another example of it.

To the families who witnessed their domestic animals dying, veterinarians told them that the deaths were probably environmentally related. What was environmentally related? Was it naturally occurring mineral water that is so prevalent in that part of the state? Was it runoff water from coal mines? Was it from gas drilling? Was it acid rain? Was it global warming? There were no answers, only more questions.

People were experiencing a hardship, not of their own doing, and they had no idea who was responsible or if anyone was. Was it an energy company for drilling? Was it Congress for the laws that limited EPA's regulatory authority?[41] Maybe it was our Creator who put the minerals such as coal, oil, and gas in the ground. No one was individually responsible. It just was. Even worse was that no one cared. I guess that is a little strong. Maybe many people cared, but it seemed liked energy independence was more important than these people. Maybe people cared, but it became clear that no one was going to do anything about it.

I met a senior citizen who lived in a small, sparsely furnished house. I remember this family so distinctly because their case was particularly sad. It was that and the fact that this kind lady kept a loaded twelve-gauge shotgun behind the front door, which I am sure she would not hesitate to use should the need arise. This woman had difficulty walking and getting around, but like many people of her generation, she kept a spotless home despite her ailments. The area was very rural, but there were about four homes close together. Some of them with suspect well water. She did not have the financial means to pay for water as some people were able to do. This woman filled pots of water from the faucet, carried them to the kitchen, and boiled the water before she would use it. I do not know if the water was potable after she boiled it, but that is what she did. She was also fortunate to receive bottled water from local people who helped her.

There was something else about this home and the people in it that will stay with me forever. Prominently displayed in the living room was a photo of a soldier and a shadow box with various awards including a Combat Infantry Badge and a Bronze Star. I knew what those medals were. My father received those same awards. This soldier was the real deal. He heard a shot fired in anger. This woman's husband fought bravely in Korea for his country: the United States of America. She, however, did not have clean water to drink. I visited many families in western Pennsylvania and West Virginia, but I was never in a warmer home than that one. I will never forget this remarkable woman, and I am humbled that I was privileged to meet her.

There were other homes and families in this area as well. A few of the people would talk with me, and others would not due to fear of reprisal. Reprisal was a real concern in this area because there were several sides of a two-sided coin when the conversation was about natural gas drilling and hydraulic fracturing. One side was the legitimate need for the United States to develop domestic energy. The September 11, 2001, attack was still a recent memory. We could not rely solely on overseas suppliers for our various energy needs. We needed our own. We needed to be independent. The September 11 attacks reaffirmed that energy independence was a concern of both the government and the energy companies.

Government officials, focused on counterterrorism efforts, recognized that America's energy grids were a legitimate terrorist target. The energy companies had plenty of examples of vandalism to their pipelines, wells, and drilling equipment in various places across the country. A close examination of these incidents revealed that they were not international terrorism. They were criminals masking themselves as environmentalists protecting a natural resource. However, it did not take much to start the fearmongering that these vandals and criminals were a credible threat to America, and they were labeled domestic terrorists. The names of Americans suspected of being capable of violence and vandalism associated with energy extraction were well known to the energy companies. Their security teams were diligent with their threat analyses and were identifying suspected criminals who were prone to acts of vandalism. However, some of these people were merely passionate and vocal about their cause. In any event, they were undoubtedly not domestic terrorists. On more than one occasion, I challenged the broad stereotypes attached to everyday people who happened to be passionate about an issue. Every day, the police deal with so many things in our country that are rooted in stereotypes and biases, and that was eerily similar to what was occurring in that rural area of America.

Another concerned group were the environmentalists who believed that natural gas drilling was destroying our environment for present and future generations. They held legitimate demonstrations, which have been embraced in this country as an acceptable way to support a cause. However, these demonstrators were viewed differently. To some, they were a bunch of activists who were standing in the way of jobs that gas drilling was bringing to these rural areas. It did not help matters that some of these people were passionate and were so radical that their words lost their effectiveness. No one, other than their followers, was listening anymore.

There were also the people who were benefiting financially from natural gas drilling. They leased their land to energy companies to drill wells and were receiving financial benefits as a result, and there were those who were employed because of the thousands of jobs that now existed. Employment was always a problem in these rural areas. Some of the people who lived there believed that gas drilling was a good thing and that the environmentalists were unreasonable. Mostly, the people I talked to were merely trying to live their lives in a peaceful area, regardless of whether they were pro-drilling or not. I knew one thing for sure, and that was that gas drilling was not going away. I also knew that there were people who needed help, and I was going to do what I could to help them, their causes aside. Armed with plenty of information, I began to research available assistance.

The first thing I learned was that the USEPA had little or no jurisdiction over much of what the people were reporting. The United States Congress, through a series of laws, delegated virtually all of the regulatory authority regarding resource extraction or gas drilling to the individual states. The USEPA retained jurisdiction to investigate pollution affecting the waters of the United States. There were suspicions of that occurring as a result of the wastewater generated from drilling and hydraulic fracturing. However, many of the allegations were not considered federal, criminal conduct. I had been around enough environmental investigations to know that proving a correlation between dead animals and pollution or its negative health effects on people was not easy. I also knew that without baseline background information about individual water wells, proving the cause of contamination would be difficult. To further complicate matters, there were no federal regulations or crimes applicable to private water wells. Few, if any, of these people had any documentation about their wells; after all, this was coal country. There could be plenty of naturally occurring contaminants in those wells or streams.

I was not thinking like a federal criminal investigator. I was thinking like a policeman, and I saw people who needed help. Finding evidence of a prosecutable crime was not as relevant as trying to get some help for these people. As I write about so often in this book, much of policing is about solving people's problems, correcting unfairness, and doing what we can to make things better.

The former director of USEPA's Criminal Investigation Division, Doug Parker, often said that we were a voice for those who had no voice. I believed that because it was consistent with what I had spent most of my career doing—helping people. I did not know what was causing their problems with drinking water, but I knew they were suffering. I did not know if the compressor stations, the hydraulic fracturing, and the flaring were putting them at risk. I just knew they had troubles, and most of them had little or no money to help themselves. These people—these Americans, these senior citizens, these family members of war heroes—needed help.

I called and visited state environmental agencies. The few who returned my calls offered no solutions because there was virtually no mechanism to assist the people with private wells in the state. I contacted the USEPA Environmental Justice (EJ) Office. I figured that if there was a miscarriage of environmental justice, it had to be in the areas I visited. However, these communities were not EJ communities as defined in the law. They needed to reside in a designated postal zip code—or a sufficient number of people needed to comprise a specific population. They did not meet either of these requirements. They were just American people. They did not meet the criteria. They did not get environmental justice. They were expendable. I even contacted a couple of energy company representatives and asked them to help low-income families in their areas. This was to no avail. I suspect that concerns about culpability posed by their lawyers quickly ended those discussions. I think a lot of the state inspectors and energy company representatives I spoke to genuinely cared about those people and wanted to help, but for various reasons, they could not and did not.

I solved similar problems as a police sergeant and state investigator, but I could not help to solve these. None of the justice-related programs such as victim witness or advocacy were applicable here. There were no crimes—or at least no prosecutable ones. However, there were indeed people in need. These people were victims, and there was no solution. There were no government programs to help these people. Some suffered through it, some were able move away, some died, and some remain in those rural areas. Some were able to hire private attorneys, but most were not. Many of the attorneys they did get did not stay around long because of the high cost of bringing an environmental lawsuit to trial. A few families may have had some limited success after years of litigation, but I doubt if any amount of money would be enough to compensate them for what they went through.

What does all of this have to do with policing? Cops chase robbers and arrest bad guys, don't they? Yes, they do that too. However, cops become a part of the community they police. They become protective of that community. When I first reported for duty to a task force in Camden, New Jersey, I believed Camden was a city of criminals. It had the highest per capita murder rate in the United States at that time. Six months after I was there, I knew that a few evil people were terrorizing the many good people who lived in that city. In a way, they were hostages because they either did not have the means or wherewithal to leave. They were good people trying to live and raise families, but they were victimized by the things happening around them. They were also expendable because as long as the crime stayed in the city and did not travel to the surrounding affluent towns, no one cared. I was experiencing in rural America what I experienced in Camden, New Jersey. People were expendable. The people were not the priority. The priorities in Camden were concerts, business, and waterfront development, and the priority in these towns in rural America was energy extraction.

It can be difficult to understand this without experiencing it like a police officer does. The average person who hears about high crime in the inner cities may believe cities are full of criminals. The reality is that there are a lot of good people who live in those cities who are often victims of circumstances beyond their control. Some people believe that people living in the energy-rich areas of rural America are either in poverty or have new tractors and barns because of their gas drilling leases. Most people have no idea what they are talking about in either case. The police do not read about it. They do not hear about it. They live it, and it becomes a part of who they are.

During a recent dinner conversation, a retired New Jersey Police Chief talked about responding to New Orleans to work the Hurricane Katrina aftermath. The chief remarked on how natural it was to do it because it is what the police do. We help people. He said that the two weeks he spent in New Orleans working that assignment was one of the most rewarding of his career. In only two weeks, he became a part of the community and was one with the people who lived there. He said that he would do it again in an instant.

Policing is about people, and we become a part of the community when we police. The community-oriented policing philosophies of the 1990s were not wrong. The administration of the program was wrong. Community-oriented policing was the policing my grandfather lived in the early twentieth century. He was vested in his community, which was the neighborhood he patrolled, and the people who lived and worked there were vested in him. It was a partnership. Over the years I have heard police executives say that community-oriented policing was partly unsuccessful because it moved cops too far away from their primary policing missions. There may be some truth to that, but in my view, the more significant reason that community-oriented policing became derailed is because it was a way for lazy cops to get off shift work and avoid answering calls for service. Instead of a building block between the community and the police, the program divided the police and did little to help the community. Today, we are seeing a resurgence of community-oriented policing that is working. It does not solve all of the problems, but the people believe that the police are doing what they can, and the police know that they are doing everything they can. The police do not solve everything. They are not able to protect everyone. They try all the time, and they experience the same frustration as the community when they cannot get it done. That is exactly what I experienced in rural America.

The interesting thing about situations similar to what I describe in this chapter is the different perspectives from which we view them. I do not have an opinion on the ongoing controversy regarding our southern border. Frankly, I do not know enough about it. There is the perspective of the people trying to emigrate from countries to our south to find a better life in America. My grandparents did the same thing, circa 1920, when they left Italy for America. The people who live in the states on our southern border have another perspective because they live in the areas that are affected. The government has a view related to customs and immigration. Each of these entities has its priorities and self-interests related to the border issue. A unique group that I have not mentioned is the law enforcement officers stationed on our southern border.

The border patrol—and the federal, state, and local law enforcement in proximity to our border with Mexico—are experiencing the events there quite differently than anyone else. Only they see the families who have no money, are malnourished and sick, and yet somehow survived the trip across Mexico to our border. Only those law enforcement officers see the dozens of people packed in the back of a truck and smuggled across the border. They observe the smells, sickness, and dead bodies. Law enforcement uncovers the drugs, the guns, and the criminals crossing the border that are destined for our cities and towns. Each of us whether liberal or conservative, government or nongovernment, and of different races, colors, and religions sees the border issue from a certain perspective. The law enforcement officer sees it all. She sees everyone's perspective and is at the epicenter of the issue, experiencing it as it happens. It becomes a part of her as she experiences it from a perspective that is both unexplainable and unknowing by anyone else. Jason Piccolo, a former Immigration and Customs Enforcement and Border Patrol agent, spent much of his career there. He recently said that a quick trip alone is not sufficient to get an education about what happens at the border.

Law enforcement officers experience life in our cities and towns similarly. The rest of us base our perspectives and positions on what we think about an issue. They are rooted in our own priorities, self-interests, and biases. The natural gas drilling in the Marcellus shale got the attention of environmentalists, many of whom did not live there. Gas drilling to them negatively impacted the world and contributed to global warming. Many of these people understood our energy needs, but they were reluctant to surrender or trade the environment for that need. The energy companies knew they now had the technology to get to the almost infinite amount of natural gas found there. They were concerned about the environment as well, but accessing those natural gas reserves was their priority. The state of Pennsylvania focused its attention on the preservation of the environment and adherence to regulations through its Department of Environmental Protection. Other state agencies focused on the continued job growth and an economy that gas drilling brought to the state. The people who lived in the drilling area had their unique focus of attention. To some, it was the economic benefits. To others, it was the environmental impact. The federal agent, who still thought like a cop, had only one focus, and that was on the people who lived there.

Just like that border law enforcement officer and the officer who is working our inner cities, I saw through and past the issues and looked directly at the people. The police look at what is happening with people and ask, "How can we help them?" Sometimes it means locking up bad actors. Sometimes it is helping to clean up a neighborhood, but mostly it is helping people navigate life's difficulties.

We do not always succeed in making a difference, but sometimes we do. Occasionally, we observe something that works out well like a child saved from dying at the border, a kid who does not become a gang member, a cleaner neighborhood, or an elderly senior citizen who gets clean water to drink. Oftentimes, these events become distant memories and are clouded by the negatives ones we experience daily.

There are times in a police officer's career when he begins to question if he is in the right job. It can happen as a result of a critical incident like a shooting. It can also happen because of the frustration that comes with the job. For example, frustration with the criminal justice system, with politicians, or from feeling that he is not accomplishing anything and is wasting his time and energy. It can happen more than once, and most of the time, we move on from it. Some cops leave policing over it.

It happened to me in rural America. People had problems, but there was little I was able to do to help them. However, police officers who are vested in their communities and vested in the people they serve are not satisfied leaving the problem the same way they found it. Cops want to make it better. We see it almost every day. Cops change flat tires, buy homeless people meals, and help people find places to live. Sometimes we cannot do anything about a problem, and we have to move on from it. The people stay with us forever though. We never forget them.

Regardless, we never stop trying, and when we do not succeed, we try again the next time—and the next time. It is who we are. Every cop reading these words has done it and will do it again because policing is about people. It is that simple.

CHAPTER SIX

THE MILITARIZATION
OF THE POLICE

The police and military have very different missions, and although there may be some mutual benefit, they must remain separate. Civilian police departments need to be very wary of confusing the public with the perception that there are similarities, because there are few.

Chapter 6
The Militarization of the Police

I was a domestic violence task force commander for several years in Camden, New Jersey. Our duty uniforms were a black battle dress. We bloused our boots and carried our equipment visibly on our belts. Our personnel were teamed up with Camden City officers and handled most of the domestic disturbances in the city while we were working. Part of my responsibilities included meeting with members of the community.

At one particular meeting, I was approached by a senior citizen who asked if she could speak with me. She wanted to thank our officers for helping her city but asked me why we needed to look so mean. When I asked her to explain what she meant, she explained that the black uniforms were intimidating as were the way my pants were tucked into the top of my boots. I told her there was not much I could do about the black uniforms, but I asked her if it would help if I untucked my pants from my boots. She thought it would.

I knew where the bloused boots came from. Soldiers wore leggings to keep their trousers from becoming tangled and trapping them in wire, brush, and other obstacles. My father wore them and said that every soldier hated the leggings. The bloused boots evolved from the leggings. During my service as a security policeman in the United States Air Force, we bloused our boots, and I hated it too. Every chance we could, we would un-blouse them.

I am not speaking for tactical teams that have a legitimate and similar reason as the military for wearing them, but there is little functional reason for officers handling calls for service to wear their trousers bloused over their boots. Even if there ever is a need, it is infrequent. Quite frankly, the reason we wear them like that is to portray a tactical or military appearance. We even buy special tactical trousers with multiple pockets that are made to be bloused over our boots.

So at roll call the night after that particular meeting, I advised our officers that in an attempt to appear less intimidating, we would no longer blouse our boots. The troops were not happy about the decision, and I am sure some of them did not comply. However, I believed that it was a small price to pay if we could change perceptions for the better.

The Posse Comitatus Act[42] (the Act) is an excellent place to start a discussion about whether civilian police are increasingly becoming militarized. The early framers of the Constitution were very detailed as they developed the laws that would govern the nation. They specifically guarded protections against government intrusions, and soon after the Constitution was ratified, they enacted a series of amendments that further defined those protections. This book is focused on one of those amendments: the fourth.

The Constitutional authors were especially concerned that the government could use military troops against the civilian population as had occurred in the colonies. They wanted to be safe and secure in their possessions against unreasonable searches and seizures. Sound familiar? The early colonists lived through bad times when British troops had virtually unlimited authority over civilian populations. The troops subjected the people to warrantless arrests and searches, and they commandeered private homes for military housing. The Act is a tangible expression of the American tradition of preventing government intrusion.

Although written to keep federal troops out of civilian homes, it applies to more than that. The Act specifically prohibits the military from direct engagement in the enforcement of civilian law. However, the Act can be overridden if determined necessary by the president or the Congress for emergent situations that require federal military assistance. That has occurred in the past during natural emergencies and threats to our country. Even during these rare events, the military's role is usually in support of civilian law enforcement. It does not replace civil authority.

The United States Army and Air Force are military service branches of the Department of Defense. A state's militia or national guard is not. Individual state army and air guard units are a function of the executive branch of a state and report to the governor. The Act does not apply to these state organizations. It only applies to the military. The police message is clear and codified in law. That is, the military and civilian police have separate functions that must remain so. The police and military have very different missions, and although there may be some mutual benefit, they must remain separate. Civilian police departments need to be very wary of confusing the public with the perception that there are similarities because there are few.

Often police departments are referred to as quasi-military or paramilitary. They have similar rank structures and chains of command, and their officers carry firearms. Interestingly, a close examination of military branches may surprisingly reveal that most personnel are not combatants. For instance, although all are trained to a basic level with firearms, most military personnel go to work just as if they were in civilian jobs. They are truck drivers, electricians, store clerks, and police. They are our civilian workforce in military uniform. We are proud of the fact that our military is comprised mostly of the ordinary, everyday people of our country and not just professional soldiers.

The Uniform Code of Military Justice (UCMJ) which applies to all members of the military is also different. It is military law.

Although many of its provisions are similar to the United States Constitution, its application is very different. Police agencies may need to remind themselves of the difference. A marine, soldier, sailor, or airman can be ordered to do something by a military police officer. They must show identification when requested and could be cited for any number of violations, including uniform and grooming standards. Try that as a civilian police officer.

The appearance of our military is different from traditional police officers. The military has wide-ranging mission responsibilities throughout the world that require different equipment and uniforms. I was a United States Air Force security policeman assigned to the Strategic Air Command. I went to work every day and checked out an M-16 rifle and 108 rounds of ammunition in six magazines which I attached to my web belt. During alerts, which were frequent in SAC, I wore a flak vest and a helmet. We wore heavily pressed and starched uniforms, and our boots were shined and bloused. No one else in the Air Force wore a uniform like that. We were different. There are similar differences in the various units of each branch of the military. Combatant and support units have a wide range of uniforms and equipment. We carried the M-16, but the aircraft mechanics carried tool bags.

The police, on the other hand, have one mission. They are responsible for protecting and serving the citizens of their communities. The police have many different tasks and objectives that support that mission such as patrol, investigations, and traffic, but the mission remains the same. Specialized units such as special weapons and tactics, tactical equipment and mission specialists, and marine operations all function in support of the protect and serve mission. Sometimes the police have a legitimate mission need to use equipment or employ tactics that are similar to those used in the military, but the similarities stop there. The police are not the military.

At the end of every war, the military surpluses equipment. Post-Vietnam and into the 1970s and 1980s, military equipment was turned over to civilian police departments for their use. Police departments received military surplus night-vision equipment, vehicles, and even firearms. Although there was a prohibition on sharing some of this equipment for a few years, today's police departments obtain various types of military equipment for both training and mission needs.

Hence, the militarization of the police, if you want to call it that, is not a new concept. For many years, the military has been sharing its equipment and knowledge with Americans, including the police. However, most of this sharing of equipment and knowledge was limited to special operations units such as SWAT teams and narcotics units and not to patrol officers. Since most citizens come in contact with patrol officers and not SWAT and narcotics teams, if patrol officers start to take on a military appearance, the public is going to take notice.

Historically, M-16 rifles were sent to police departments, but most of them are long gone and have been replaced with more functional firearms. Newer firearms, although still built on the original ArmaLite[43] plans, have evolved for today's police operations. Some of this equipment was developed and tested by the military and is now available as civilian models for police use. They have optics that enable the operator to see distances, and in low-light situations, laser-sighting systems and suppressors. Since September 11, they are standard in most police departments. They look a lot like military firearms, but they are not. They are civilian market models.

Police firearms have become a hotly debated topic partly because of the broader national debate on firearms and partly because of the militarization of police discussion. It is worth taking a closer look at the evolution of police firearms to understand how and why we got where we are now. The military was certainly an influence, but is not the only factor.

Traditionally, police officers in the United States were armed with a .38 caliber revolver, which was a reliable handgun for most applications. Longer-barrel versions were carried by uniformed officers, and the shorter, highly concealable snub-noses, were carried by plainclothes officers. Ammunition for the .38 caliber and its slightly more powerful .38 Special was widely available and reasonably priced for police departments. Colt[44] and Smith & Wesson[45] manufactured most of these standard six-shot revolvers that the police carried. These handguns were reliable because they operated mechanically, the frame was heavy enough to handle the ammunition without substantial recoil, and although primarily short distance firearms, they could be accurate to fifty yards and beyond. Police officers routinely fired for a score at fifty-yard targets with the revolver. A trained shooter could learn to reload the pistol quickly using a two-round method, and the later introduction of the speed loader enabled a reload of six rounds all at once. The .38 caliber revolver served law enforcement well, and although it is no longer carried by most officers, it is occasionally still seen on an officer's hip.

Police augmented the .38 caliber police sidearm with the twelve-gauge shotgun. Not all officers were armed with this firearm, and they were not always readily available. Some were locked in storage rooms at station houses and issued if needed. Later, they were mounted in patrol vehicles and became more the norm. Rarely were the police armed with any firearms beyond the basic police revolver or maybe the shotgun. The few fully automatic weapons that were available such as the early Thompson[46] and later submachine guns such as the Colt[47] and H&K[48] were in specialized units, and the average police officer was never even trained on them.

The semiautomatic pistol was around for a long time as the military adopted the .45 caliber automatic Colt[49] pistol as its issue sidearm early in the twentieth century. The military, however, did not intend for the pistol to be a soldier's primary firearm. That was the job of the rifle. The handgun was carried in specialized assignments by pilots, headquarters staff, some infantry troops, and even military police. The United States Air Force security police moved away from the .45 automatic to the .38 caliber early, although other services, such as the army, retained it until the nine-millimeter replaced it. Those who used the .45 tell plenty of stories about its field performance, challenges managing recoil, and the difficulty firing it. Although it was a military standard-issue sidearm for many years, it never gained popularity with civilian police. This has changed slightly—but not in numbers comparable to other calibers.

The police did not embrace semiautomatic pistols early. The .38 revolver was proven reliable, and it left our police inventories slowly. The police were never generally gun people. To cops, the firearm was merely a necessary tool. The .357 magnum that became popular and that I carried early on was issued as an effort to give us more firepower, which it did. What it did not do was give us the higher-capacity ammunition capabilities that the later semiautomatic handguns provided. Also, the ammunition was expensive and produced a significant amount of recoil. Some departments opted to carry .38 caliber ammunition in the .357 Magnum, which defeated the whole purpose—if there was any validity to it in the first place.

The 1980s began a series of law enforcement firearms changes that continue to this day. The police began to focus on a theory of multiple-target threats that seriously outgunned them. The police addressed this problem by adopting the high-capacity magazine semiautomatic pistol.

There were many reasons for the changes in police handguns, but a couple of significant ones probably contributed as much to the change as any other single event. The FBI shootout in South Florida[50] was one, and the later North Hollywood Bank of America robbery[51] was another. Criminals in these events were armed with automatic weapons, but the law enforcement officers were mainly armed only with revolvers. During both of these events, robbers with high-velocity firearms and body armor overwhelmed the police. The bravery of the officers at both incidents determined the outcomes but not without serious casualties.

These two events prompted some police departments to provide officers with patrol rifles. This also began the policing departure from six-shot revolvers to semiautomatic pistols to address multiple threats. We developed some teaching philosophies designed to give officers an edge in confrontations. We saw shooting techniques change to combat stances and equipment suggestions such as horizontally mounted magazine pouches, backup guns, and knives. Today's handgun configuration looks like something out of a science fiction movie, and when carried in the leg rig, it has little resemblance to traditional police equipment.

These events and changes evolved into the firearms configurations we see carried by many police officers today. We see large semiautomatic pistols with high-capacity magazines, laser sights, and mounted lights in hip- or leg-mounted tactical holsters. Many departments have returned to nine-millimeter handguns after favoring the .40 caliber for some years.

Many police agencies moved to the .40 caliber because it was slightly heavier with better terminal ballistics. Departments returned to the nine-millimeter for several reasons. One reason is the cost of ammunition. Ammunition for the nine-millimeter is manufactured more than any other handgun ammunition and is thus the cheapest. Another reason is that ammunition research and development has become highly evolved, and there is plenty of nine-millimeter ammunition on the market today, producing satisfactory terminal ballistics for police use. Finally, the .40 caliber semiautomatic pistol was sometimes difficult for officers to manage. Its slightly larger size, significant recoil, and tendency for muzzle flip created challenges, and many officers were happy to see it replaced with the nine-millimeter. There was another reason the .40 caliber semiautomatic handgun gained widespread use, and it had a lot to do with marketing. Police departments moved to these guns because the manufacturers did a great job selling them. Departments like new and innovative equipment, and it did not take much for the .40

caliber semiautomatic handgun to catch on. It was not until much later that we saw the trade back to the nine-millimeter.

Fast forward to September 11, 2001, when this country experienced something on a magnitude that most of us had never seen. We saw bombings of buildings before, but the September 11 attack was a coordinated, militaristic, multipronged one. Foreign terrorists attacked America, and there were real threats to the security of our country. We witnessed everyday Americans volunteering to be a part of the defense from future attacks and the recovery from the initial one. People from across the United States went to the World Trade Center to sift through the rubble. They went to the Pentagon and to Somerset County, Pennsylvania. They flew on airplanes prepared to thwart the next hijacking. They enlisted in our military at a rate that we had not seen since the Pearl Harbor attack of December 7, 1941. The police got in on the action as well. Since September 11, 2001, civilian police have been preparing for battle.

The police stepped into the role of a militia and adopted much of what goes along with that connotation. The police thought that way, dressed that way, equipped themselves that way, and trained that way. It all made sense. No other civilian branch of government was going to step into that role and fill the void that everyone agreed was there. The police already considered themselves quasi-military and began to militarize more fully.

The police would step up and defend us against the attack we all feared was coming. The police would stand in the gap until relieved by the military. Some would point out that this happened before, during the drug wars of the 1980s, when the police used military equipment and tactics in counter-drug operations. It also happened when a few departments converted surplus military vehicles for urban assault operations. Both of these examples are true, but they were confined mostly to specialized units such as narcotics and Special Weapons and Tactics (SWAT). The average blue suits still looked like they always did.

Immediately after September 11, many officers and departments saw themselves as the defenders of the country, a slightly different slant on the service to their communities that they swore to. The government helped in this phenomenon by issuing or providing grants for gas masks, patrol rifles, more ammunition, and other equipment. Officers started to dress differently as well. The well-pressed, creased trousers gave way to the pants that bloused over the boots that now replaced the low-quarter shoes. We put away the traditional police uniform and replaced it with a utility one or battle dress utility one. It had more pockets to carry all of the stuff we now had with us. We wore tactical boots—first black ones and then desert camouflage.

We removed our ballistic panels from our concealed carriers and placed them in a tactical carrier that we wore on the outside of the uniform shirt. Our soft body armor or vest became tactical outer carriers and kits. These new carriers were similar to the Modular Lightweight Load-carrying Equipment (MOLLE) systems used by the military. They were highly functional and enabled us to carry additional ammunition for both our handguns and rifles. We attached first aid kits, which we now called IFAKs, tourniquets, and flashlights. I guess the only thing I have not seen on the modern-day police officer is an MRE.[52]

The tactical leg or thigh holster emerged from use solely by SWAT teams to everyday police officers. The magazine pouches moved from vertical to horizontal. There were legitimate reasons for both the leg holster and the movement of magazine pouches. The tactical carriers that we were now wearing on the outside of our uniforms made it difficult to draw the pistol or access magazines. The solution was these two pieces of equipment. The leg or thigh holster, by the way, gained popularity with tactical teams for the same reason because they traditionally wore heavy body armor in a carrier and on the outside of the uniform. The cop who had his boots bloused, magazine pouch mounted horizontally, and a thigh rig holster was easily recognizable as high-speed, low drag, and tactical.

American police prepared for war, and ultimately the evolution of uniforms and equipment proved to be useful, especially in active shooter events.

The service cap or cover, the most recognizable identifier of a police officer besides the badge, was gone too. The baseball cap, helmet, or no cover at all replaced it. Ties became a thing of the past. We wore black gloves that were no longer filled with lead, and they now had the legitimate purpose of protecting us from sharp objects and were certainly not less menacing. The only resemblance of the police uniform was the blue or sheriff's department green, but even that became adulterized by black, desert camouflage, green, and desert tan. The uniforms were functional, the equipment was better, and the training was sound. Most departments, working with tight equipment budgets, cannot afford to have multiple uniforms, and in some cases, the utility uniform was cheaper.

September 11 changed policing methodology, and the changes were not necessarily bad. They were just different. It was also one of the reasons the patrol rifle gained widespread acceptance and became part of standard-issue police firearms. Forget about the fact that we lost a bunch of cops who were outgunned in South Florida many years before that. Forget about the fact that the LAPD faced superior firepower in the Bank of America robbery in North Hollywood.[53] Shot, and sometimes dead, cops did not put us in the military mind-set, but the dastardly deeds on September 11 sure did.

Ultimately, the attack never came. That does not mean that we were wrong to prepare for it. Quite the contrary, the incredible work at all levels of law enforcement produced the intelligence necessary to thwart another attack. Federal, state, and local law enforcement coordinated resources like never before to ensure that it did not. Furthermore, we experienced violence by deranged individuals who claimed to be acting in support of international terrorism. Because we prepared, our police officers were trained and equipped to respond to that violent carnage.

Even though a similar September 11 attack never came, some officers and departments with the militia persona did not return to what they were before that fateful day. The uniforms, equipment, and training that were developed to prepare for the war that never came remained. It stayed because it benefited the police, most cops liked the setup, and it was functional. Today, we often see police officers dressed in what some would call a Class B, tactical, or utility uniform. The reality is that the uniform configurations we see now are necessary because of the amount of equipment cops are forced to carry. However, the police who are wearing these uniforms need to be cognizant of the perceptions they create in the minds of the public.

The appearance of police cars has also changed a number of times over the years. We went from unmarked to marked in limitless combinations. There were sound reasons every time we made a change. The stealth packages, as we called them, have taken on a whole new significance. The black and whites that were highly recognizable on the West Coast were set aside years ago on the East Coast. Now we see all black cars, blue cars, and SUVs with suppressed identifications on the side. What happened to the highly recognizable original color schemes that were designed to be that way? We now have tactical, militaristic-looking vehicles that accompany the uniforms and equipment.

The adoption of military-like equipment, uniforms, and vehicles ultimately benefitted police operations, especially in their new role as active shooter responders. However, we are still left with the discussion that the Constitution prohibits the militarization of the police. The police are not soldiers. They are not the military, but they can learn from the lessons learned by the military. We can enjoy a civilian police-military cooperation without blurring the lines.

The United States military has a long history of perfecting things like training, equipment, and tactics during both preparedness and mission deployments that have tremendous value beyond their original intended purpose. If you want to get a high-intensity workout, buy lessons from a former Navy SEAL[54] about learning to get fit. If you are a corporate executive and want to learn how to lead people, there are any number of training events presented by retired military command officers. Outdoor enthusiasts looking for cold-weather gear can probably thank the US military for developing it. That Willys-Overland[55] quarter-ton 4x4 utility truck would never be the Jeep[56] many people enjoy driving today if it were not for the US military.

The military has a tremendous need to recruit and train people with wide-ranging skill sets who can be promoted as leaders. The military has mission-essential needs, and corporate America, through its tremendous manufacturing capability, develops the equipment needed to meet these needs. The military develops mission capabilities through its order of battle, strategic, and tactical operations. There are lessons for civilian police departments in all of these. They are not, however, specific operational procedures.

Sometimes the police are tasked with doing things they have no training for or equipment to use, and they are not prepared to do it. That may be a result of assumptions that come with the military-like appearance police have adopted or because there is simply no one else to do the task. Too often, law enforcement—either on their own or through ill-conceived plans—are the only people available and are selected for something they should not be doing. We see it in investigative agencies all of the time. Talented plainclothes investigators will don body armor, handguns in tactical holsters, or a shotgun or rifle to execute a search warrant under circumstances where there is a great potential for violence. Most of the time, these investigators are poorly prepared for those entries. Instead, well-trained tactical units should be conducting them. Most of the time, these situations end without incident, but sometimes they do not. My own personal guidance on this issue has developed over a career and is this. If specialized equipment and specialized training is needed to do something, someone else needs to do it. In New Jersey, for instance, we rarely see these kinds of warrants executed without a specialized tactical team.

As an example of lessons learned, my father described an event that occurred early during World War II. General MacArthur had begun his "I Shall Return" campaign. He attacked the Japanese in the jungles of New Guinea with an inadequately trained and ill-equipped division of the US Army. The American division suffered heavy casualties against the entrenched Japanese defenders. My father was assigned to an infantry regiment stationed in the Panama Canal Zone at the time, the site that would later become the US Army's jungle warfare school. Those men in the canal zone heard about the battle of New Guinea and knew the troops there were unprepared for the battle. They had neither the training nor the equipment for jungle warfare. My father always believed that the Army's Panama Department jungle warfare troops should have fought the New Guinea campaign and not the inadequately trained and equipped division that did. To my father's dying day, he recalled that battle by saying, "The army should have sent us to New Guinea." I only understood much later what he meant. My father would go to war, experience the horrors of it, and come to know how unprepared those troops were for what they were sent to do.

Occasionally in policing, a job will go bad, and people will get hurt. When we execute a search or arrest warrant, violence resulting in serious injury or death to both the police and the suspects can occur. With no intent to second-guess anyone's actions, we have to ask ourselves whether we were trained and equipped to do the job. Sometimes the answer is yes, and the result is the same. Sometimes, however, the answer is different, and a better course of action would have been more appropriate. We cannot change what occurred, but we can always strive to be better the next time.

With regard to the militarization of police, training also enters into the discussion. We now depend on officers to respond to situations well beyond their normal operational responsibilities. In this day of mass murder and widespread violence, it has become necessary to evolve our training to meet that need. Some of the training we now provide to officers was historically only provided to specialized units such as SWAT. We did not teach our officer tactics specifically. However, neither did we ask our officers to handle active shooter calls alone.

Before the Columbine High School shooting[57] in 1999, we taught officers to arrive on those scenes and hold them down until a specialized team could arrive. That is no longer the case. Currently, we expect our officers to enter those hostile fire zones and take action to neutralize the shooter. We have learned some basic tactical skills from the military that are useful for these events, and we now teach them to our officers. These skills will also help keep our officers safe during everyday police service.

Essentially, what appears militaristic to some is merely a further development of police training programs that continue to evolve as we learn more about keeping officers safe while accomplishing specific objectives. Civilian police use-of-force instructors have the difficult job of trying to find ways to prepare officers for these rare violent events.

Use-of-force instructors, motivational speakers, and former military personnel use the term *warrior* for the same purposes we use the terms *sheep, sheepdogs,* and *wolves.* We are trying to create the mind-set of preparing for battle. The word *battle* is what gets people's attention and causes them to object and cry foul. The police are not combatants. We are preparing for battle. We are okay with the police being protectors or guardians, but we do not want warriors among the ranks of our police. It sounds too militaristic and brings to mind images of Sun Tzu,[58] samurais, knights, military combat troops, and even SWAT members. It represents interpersonal aggression and produces fear in people even if we consciously know that may not be the case. We think of warriors as attackers moving to the fight and inflicting mayhem in their wake. The perception becomes our reality. The word *guardian*, however, strikes a different chord with us.

Guardian brings to mind images of angels, quiet vigilant strength, a watchful eye, and a sheepdog. The guardian is our best friend and our protector all rolled into one. Rather than producing fear in people, the guardian gives us a sense of safety, peacefulness, and even serenity. We think of the warrior as the soldier and the guardian as the police officer. Lately, the word *protector* has emerged as a replacement for warrior. Somebody decided that protector is more aligned with what police officers are, and this terminology is gaining momentum. We want a police guardian and not a warrior soldier protecting our neighborhoods. I write more about these word associations in a future chapter on recruitment, hiring, and training.

The terms here are meaningless to a police instructor. The terms are only the vehicle I am using to get the officer to think. The terms used in training are designed to provoke thought and actions in whatever form is easily understood. If we sound softer and more approachable to the public we serve by calling ourselves protectors or guardians, I am all for it. Recall my encounter with the lady who did not like my black uniform and bloused boots. There is a problem with this line of thinking, and it is this. When a police officer engages in a violent encounter because some predator wants to do harm, it is a battle, and we need that cop to be a warrior—and not a protector or a guardian.

I recently read a *Los Angeles Times* story that indicated that the Transportation Security Administration (TSA) is preparing to deploy more floppy-eared dogs. According to the article, during a tour of Washington's Dulles International Airport, TSA Administrator David Pekoske said, "We find the passenger acceptance of floppy-ear dogs is just better. It presents just a little bit less of a concern, and doesn't scare children."[59] Some law enforcement social media feeds were critical of this and joked that we are now working to demilitarize our canines. I found the response humorous and got a chuckle out of it, but at the same time, I like the idea. Anytime we can change the public's perception that the police are overly militaristic, we should be open to doing it.

The TSA probably has the most difficult public relations challenges of any agency. They deal with millions of people in an adversarial manner every single day. They need to enforce security while keeping the system moving at the same time. They receive plenty of complaints about everything from slow lines to their treatment of the public. They also use canines to look for contraband, primarily explosives, carried by passengers. This often appears to be intrusive and intimidating—even if we accept that it is necessary. What is wrong with doing it in a less intimidating manner if it does not compromise the mission or its personnel? What is wrong with a police department acknowledging that perceptions matter and, where possible and without compromising officer safety, taking those perceptions under consideration? Sometimes it is not possible to change the way we look, the tools we use, or the way we conduct an operation. Sometimes it looks intimidating because police operations can be a scary business. However, when possible, we should consider perceptions and make changes.

My neighbor has two large, muscular dogs with pointed ears. They patrol (my description) his yard like they are sentries. They are near my vineyard, and anytime I go out there, the dogs sit erect. Their ears are rigid, and they carefully watch what is going on around them. Sometimes they run up to the property line. The first few times this happened, it was unsettling, and quite frankly, it still is. If they were Labrador retrievers, I doubt I would feel the same way. The thing is, on the rare occasion when they do come over, they are very friendly and love to play. I am sure they are capable of delivering a severe bite. However, the dogs no longer concern me because I have come to trust that they are not a threat. My perception of them, based on what they look like, changed.

If we accept that implicit bias exists in many of us, and we cite it as one possible reason for police judgment decisions, then we must also accept that the same exists in people. People perceive things, and sometimes that perception becomes a reality. A white, bloused-booted, uniform-wearing officer with a crushed hat could be perceived as militaristic no matter the reality because to that person his perception is reality. On more than one occasion, police have been called jackbooted thugs because of the way they looked or carried their equipment.

An FBI operation in South Florida was recently scrutinized by Congress. The FBI arrested a person who was indicted as part of the 2016 presidential election investigation. Some people believe that the operation was heavy-handed and that the show of force was excessive and militaristic because of the number of agents, vehicles, and weapons involved. The reality is that the FBI and many other law enforcement agencies conduct operations like that daily. Why did this one attract attention? Why was it so heavily scrutinized? I believe it is because there are people who have strong opinions on both sides of that investigation. Their opinions influence other people's perceptions of the way the FBI handled the arrest. It is less about what the FBI did and more about what people think should or should not have happened to the person arrested in this high-profile election investigation. The news media cameras present when the FBI arrived to serve the warrant did not help matters. This is an excellent example of how perception is affected by beliefs.

The military has been a source of a lot of different kinds of training that support various police operations. I noted earlier that following September 11, many people joined the military because they wanted to defend America. Some of those enlistees served in special operations units and have since separated from the military. Some are now trainers for either federal, state, or local governments or private contractors. Some are now civilian police officers. They teach beneficial information to law enforcement, usually in tactics or firearms. This is nothing new. The military has supported civilian law enforcement training for many years. I have trained with, and have been trained by, some of the best special forces troops the military produced so I support this entirely, with one proviso. A civilian law enforcement use-of-force instructor must monitor the training to ensure the information being taught is consistent with civilian law, policies, and procedures. As I have consistently written, we can learn from military operations, but we are not the military. We are the police.

Military operations grab our attention—specifically those units that conduct tactical operations. No one wants to watch a movie or read a book about supply, maintenance, or administrative units or about the average soldier, sailor, or marine doing the vital work they do every day. We want to read about or watch the exploits of those special operations units that do the incredible work they are called upon to do. That is what captures our attention. It is who we are as Americans. Is it any wonder then that our police officers, who are already carrying military-like equipment and have a tactical mindset, easily adopt that persona as well? We have positioned them to do precisely that.

The special weapons and tactics team or the tactical equipment and mission specialists are highly visible when they are deployed. They make great photos, but they are there for a specific mission assignment that the police are called upon to perform. They are not the normalness of policing. Policing is not SWAT and special tactics units. They are the everyday people who come from the rank-and-file citizenry of our country who decide they want to be police officers. Most of their day is spent answering calls for service, and most of them turn out to be civil complaints that do not involve arresting criminals. Every good cop I have ever known, no matter how specialized their careers have become, regards the everyday patrol officer as the essence of policing.

I had many conversations with my father about the military. Most of those conversations were not about battles. They were about baseball and beer. They were about soldiers. However, on occasion, he briefly talked about war, and when he did, it was a measured conversation. I could almost see the memories on his face. My father heard a shot fired in anger, and his most coveted award was the Combat Infantry Badge (CIB) because of everything the award represented. My father explained that supplies and support personnel won battles, and we would talk about the many military personnel required to field one combat troop. How many military support personnel from all branches supported the small group of Navy SEALS who captured Osama Bin Laden? It is hard to get to the answer unless we take into account the supply clerks, refuelers, maintenance people, and electronics personnel who supported the operation. The "sexy" is what captures our attention, which is understandable because those combat troops and special operators are in harm's way and warrant our attention and gratitude.

The militaristic appearance of police officers is not what policing is about. Instead, it represents a specific necessity in police operations. Officers may respond to a private residence and help save a young person who overdosed. They may also respond to a public place such as a school, a house of worship, or a hospital to confront a violent offender engaged in the mass murder of innocent people. We rely on police officers who may be inadequately trained and often ill-equipped to stop violence. Police officers will go alone and outgunned into harm's way to save innocent people. The uniform, equipment, and training have all evolved to help officers respond to all of these wide-ranging responsibilities.

Some officers like the aura that surrounds the military and, more specifically, military special operations personnel. I continue to be amazed by this fascination with the tactical because it never held an interest for me, but that is the diversity that exists in people, including cops. Although it certainly has its place in police operations because tactically sound officers are safe officers, it does not represent the normalness of policing. A police department's effectiveness depends on many factors, and tactical operations is only one of them. Our good officers possess many skills that together make them successful and safe, and one of those skills is sound tactics.

The police should consider the perceptions created by appearance, equipment, and demeanor. They should recognize that these things create the impression of militarization, and, where possible, they should work to lessen them. On the other hand, the police are not the military, and the public should recognize that despite what they see, which may appear to be militaristic. The police are fortunate to be able to use lessons learned from the military to do a better job. The police are a part of the people they serve. They are not an army of occupation.

CHAPTER SEVEN

MENTAL HEALTH
AND RESILIENCY

A man kneeling on one knee met me when I arrived. His clothes were tattered, torn, and smoking. He was reaching out to me with one hand. He had no face, but yet he spoke to me and said, "Help my sister."

Chapter 7
Mental Health and Resiliency

A book about the police being the people must include a discussion on health, well-being, and resilience. We are losing more cops to suicide, alcohol, poor health, and other substances than to felonious assaults. According to the Officer Down Memorial page, a nonprofit organization that tracks line-of-duty deaths, 148 law enforcement officers died in the line of duty in 2018,[60] and 59 percent of those deaths were the result of felonious assaults against officers, and 41 percent were by other means such as motor vehicle crashes, heart attacks, and other accidental causes. In 2018, there were 160 known police suicides according to Karen Solomon, president and founder of Blue HELP.[61] That number does not account for every suicide—only the ones that were confirmed. We can be reasonably sure that there are suicides that agencies do not report and deaths, that although reported as accidental, were in fact suicides. We are killing ourselves at a higher rate than the bad guys, and that is just in suicide deaths. It does not account for the early deaths of cops who are caused by a lifetime of unhealthy habits.

Police line-of-duty death determinations seem, at least on their face, to be easy to understand, but upon closer examination of how officers die, we see that it is not that simple. Officers killed as the result of felonious assaults, such as being shot, stabbed, or beaten to death, immediately come to mind because they are line-of-duty deaths. Next are the deaths that, although non-felonious assaults, occur while the officer is in the performance of his duties. These include on-duty officer deaths from car wrecks, falls from high places, and drownings. A law enforcement agency makes these line-of-duty death determinations based upon a wide range of information about the death and the agency's criteria. Sometimes they include events that, although not explicitly caused by an on-duty event, may be directly associated with the profession such as health-related deaths from heart attacks, September 11 substance exposures, and other duty-related illnesses.

Agencies rarely determine suicides to be line-of-duty deaths. The reasons for that are not clearly defined, although there are many opinions about it. One reason is the negative stigma associated with suicide. Suicide is the death nobody wants to acknowledge or discuss. Law enforcement agencies today have no hesitation declaring that an officer who dies of a heart attack died in the line of duty, but they will not readily reach that determination for an officer who dies by his own hand. The police are supposed to be braver, stronger, and unflappable in the face of danger and somewhere approaching superhuman. A cop who falls short of that and gives up or checks out of this life on his own accord failed the system. Suicide scares the rest of us on a personal level, and it hits too close to home. Often officers who complete the act of suicide are good cops, and if they could not handle life, how close to losing it are the rest of us?

There is a known risk that we take every day on every shift that we do not talk about, but we know it is there. If one of us gets hurt or killed by a felonious assault, it is battle, and although we have a casualty, we will prevail in the battle. We will hunt down the killer and bring him or her to justice. Those responsible for the injury or death of our cops will pay for their deeds. We also know about the mental health risks associated with continuous exposure to trauma. When we see a brother or sister officer take his or her own life, we have nowhere to go with it. We cannot track down and arrest those responsible. We take stock of our misguided contributing responsibility, and it weighs on us. We cannot face the officer's family and children. We lost that battle, and there is nothing we can do about it. We handle it the same way we handle everything else in police work. We take all of the trauma and horror we see every day, and we ignore it. We do not acknowledge it. We do not talk about it, and we are certainly not going to put a flag and a plaque on it and remember it for all time. Not all agencies handle suicide this way. Some do something and acknowledge it for what it is: another police casualty. However, many do not, and the families are left with the loss of their family member who was a hero one day and not mentioned the next. So very often, that highly decorated, fondly regarded officer is so until the day he or she takes their own life and then is never spoken about again.

Our thoughts are always with the families left behind by suicide. First with the immediate family, significant others, children, and parents, but there are also the friends and colleagues who lost that person. The proud blue police family instantly becomes essentially orphaned. There is a mantra often used by Blue HELP[62] and others who understand this horror to the extent anyone can: "It is not how the officer died but how the officer lived that mattered."

There are no specific statistics to support it, but in some ways, the health of officers is improving despite the high suicide numbers. Young cops seem to be a little healthier. Many do not smoke, and they exercise regularly. While alcohol remains a big part of policing, it may not be abused as often as it was in the past. Time will be the judge of how healthy our cops are over a twenty-five or thirty-year career.

On the other hand, the ten-year cops I talk to are as predictable as ever. They are experiencing the same weariness, frustrations, and aloneness that I felt at the same time in my career. They only feel comfortable with other cops, they drink alcohol to a point necessary to sedate their feelings, and they are weary all the time. They go to work and without conscious thought generate all the energy they need to work ten- or twelve-hour shifts and overtime details. They go home exhausted, but they do not sleep. The cycle continues for days, months, and years. They do not talk about it, and if they do, it is in short blurbs. If someone listens carefully and knows what to listen for, they will hear everything I am describing.

Recently, an officer talked to me about a job he had just handled. A young female was creating a disturbance to the point that the police became involved. The female was intoxicated or under the influence of some substance and was in possession of a small amount of marijuana. This person would not comply with police commands— or could not understand them because of her intoxication—became physically combative, and was ultimately taken into custody. While in police custody, she spat on the officers who were processing her. The police charged her with assaulting the officers in addition to the other charges that initiated the police contact. The prosecutor declined prosecution of the indictable offenses and instead referred the matter to a lower court for a disposition of the charges.

With the benefit of twenty-twenty hindsight, which the Court cautioned us from using, and while comfortably seated reading this, you and I could think the prosecutor's decision was understandable. Spitting on the cops is disgusting, but she was under the influence of something. Although that does not exonerate her, maybe it does not rise to the level of a crime either. The cops were not hurt. She probably has a substance abuse problem that created the police contact in the first place. Is she a violent offender?

Look at this incident from the officers' perspectives. From the very beginning, the police do not want to be involved in this incident. This person is under the influence of something and continues to act out in the officers' presence. They do not want to arrest her, but she will not stop the disorderly conduct that is interfering with the peace and order of other members of the public. She refuses to follow, or fails to understand, their commands and resists, which requires the police to use some level of force to subdue her. The police take her to the station, and while being processed, she spits on them. No one wants to be spit on. It is an assault and not just because of bruised egos or an inflated sense of importance. No officer wants someone else's bodily fluids on them, and they take precautions to avoid it. The officers are experiencing elevated stress levels while dealing with a subject they did not want to arrest in the first place. They have soiled uniforms and are generally frustrated that the subject spat on them. They will be tied up with this person for the next several hours for processing and writing the report. The police file a charge against this individual for assaulting a police officer. Although the elements in this crime were minor because there was no injury to the officers, it is, in fact, a crime. There is no lesser charge for assaulting police officers. It was an assault, and it is a crime. The prosecutor exercises his lawful discretion and decides not to prosecute the offender and remands the matter to a lower court for judicial processing.

The prosecutor probably made the right decision. However, it is easy to understand why the police officers involved are frustrated by the whole event. They are angry because of the perceived lack of support from prosecutors who are quick to identify themselves as law enforcement. While their perception is technically not correct, to those cops, it is more than a perception. It is real. They feel abuse from both the subject involved and the criminal justice system. They feel both abandoned and alone and retreat behind the blue wall of safety.

This story is real. It happened just like I described it. Unfortunately, it is only one incident on one day. These incidents happen routinely. Police officers respond to situations similar to this one every single day. They are expected to handle situations that do not start out as a police matter but turn into one. They have few tools with which to handle these situations, and they often have no choice but to arrest even when there should be a better way. Emotions are running high for subjects and the police. They often use some level of force—usually physical or mechanical—because the subject fails to comply with police commands. They spend hours after the arrest processing the offender and completing the paperwork. Only then, with the benefit of hindsight, does a prosecutor decide that the offense does not warrant a criminal prosecution and declines to pursue it. How many times does a cop need to learn that he did everything right, but he will not be supported in his actions for doing it? Mistrust, frustration, and anger are not only the purview of the public side of the people-police equation. Those feelings apply to all of the people.

I cannot describe what burning flesh smells like, but every first responder reading this—cops, firefighters, and emergency medical personnel—will understand. The first time I smelled it, I was posted to secure the scene of an airplane crash in North Dakota. Two United States Air Force F-106s on a routine training mission from Minot Air Force Base collided in the air. One of the pilots from these single-crew aircraft ejected from his airplane and was safe. The pilot of the other airplane did not eject. He remained in the cockpit and was killed when the airplane crashed. The air force sent security policeman to the scene to secure the crash site, which included the cockpit containing the dead pilot. I was one of them.

Late at night, we arrived at the crash site to find an inverted cockpit. We really could not see much more in the darkness, and efforts to recover the pilot's remains or the aircraft were ceased until the morning. A few personnel from the base were at the site when we arrived, and they departed shortly after. Only the two of us remained there to secure the scene. We quickly observed the smell that I cannot describe. It permeated everything that was there, everything that we brought with us, and everything that we were. The next morning, a helicopter arrived with personnel to recover the dead pilot. By this time, the odor had become a part of us, and we were no longer conscious of it. Of the salvage work that I recall that day, one event has forever remained in my memory.

Another pilot from that F-106 squadron knelt onto the ground where the cockpit, now suspended by a crane cable, once rested. The pilot attempted to sift through the ground, for what I do not know. It looked like he was trying to retrieve his friend. The charred soil, the pilot's remains, and the pieces of the airplane all combined, and there was that smell. It filled the air to the point that it was everywhere. It was a part of the land and the air. It was all there was.

We spent a couple of days at that crash site. When we were relieved and got back to the barracks, I showered and did laundry. A few of us who were at the scene sat around with other cops and beers and shared what we did out there. That was pretty much the end of it. For a long time, my most vivid recollection of the event was that we had no food other than the one flight line box lunch and water we brought with us. For the first few days, the Air Force did not provide meals for us. The local Salvation Army did. I did not think any more about it, never had to go back there, and did not have dreams or nightmares.

The next time I smelled burning flesh, I was not at the scene. I was in a command post working as a communicator plotter (Complotter) in Central Security Control (CSC) at Plattsburgh Air Force Base in upstate New York. Two FB-111s from Plattsburgh on a routine training mission crashed in the mountains of Vermont. We deployed security policemen from our base at Plattsburgh for scene security. I was not deployed to the crash site. Instead, I remained in the CSC and coordinated our communications with the site through a direct radio link we were able to establish. Before that radio link, we were working through the New York and Vermont State Police and had no direct communications with our personnel at the scene. Once our voice communications were established, and I was able to speak directly with our cops on the scene, I knew what those on-scene troops were experiencing. I was not there, but at the same time, I was. That odor that I cannot describe filled the CSC. It did not last long, and I did not think much more about it. I had a few beers when we got off duty and never mentioned it to anyone. I did not have bad dreams or nightmares about it. It was a nonevent.

One afternoon in 1985, I was working my assignment as the police department's emergency management operations officer. Hurricane Gloria had just brushed the east coast of New Jersey, and since we experienced little more than some high winds, the state remained unscathed. We had prepared for wind and rain, and I worked all night and remained ready if we were needed. While sitting at the communications desk, talking to a dispatcher and thinking about going home, a call came in of a reported explosion. I responded from the station, and for whatever reason, I was the first unit at the scene. A man kneeling on one knee met me when I arrived. His clothes were tattered, torn, and smoking. He was reaching out to me with one hand. He had no face, but he spoke to me and said, "Help my sister." She was in the house. He looked like a dead man reaching out from the grave, like the people you see in low-budget horror movies. And then there was that smell that I knew. I got on the radio and said that I did not know what I had but to send help. My radio transmission, in and of itself, is evidence of how bad the situation was that day. Cops will ask for another unit, or fire or medical assistance, but they do not radio for help. I did that day. Cops who heard my radio transmission would later tell me they knew by my voice inflection that there was a problem. They had never heard me like that.

There was no evidence of an explosion or fire—only a quiet calm in the area. I do not know how I knew where to look for the sister, but I went into the house and found her standing in the bathroom shower. She had gone into the house and into the shower to extinguish the flames. I knew that smell. She did not speak to me. She seemed to recognize my uniform and went along with me and the firefighters who had by now arrived at the scene.

Whatever personal survival system I was operating under is anyone's guess. I called for a helicopter because I knew these people were in trouble. The storm still had the New Jersey State Police medevac grounded, so the Delaware State Police responded for the evacuation. The firefighters and medical personnel did everything possible to save that brother and sister. They both died a few days apart in the burn unit at Chester Crozier Hospital.

Our preliminary investigation determined that the explosion was from the home's underground nuclear fallout shelter, which had been built in the early 1960s. Propane from a leaking underground pipeline entered the shelter drains and filled the room with explosive levels of gas. The man and his sister went into the shelter to see if there was storm damage because the property was for sale. The man lit a match and ignited the invisible gas.

I guess I worked about a million hours on that job. I know I did not go home for a couple of days and had already worked the previous night because of the hurricane. I do not recall if the nightmares started during that first night's sleep, but they started. The nightmare is always the same. The man is reaching out from the grave and calling out to me for help. I cannot help him. They do not occur all the time. They did not happen every night back then, but just like the smell, they are there.

At the outset of this book, I assured readers that I was not going to tell a bunch of war stories because I do not want to talk about them, and no one wants to hear them. However, that story so clearly demonstrates how trauma invades an officer's life and affects his well-being. A trained mental health professional would have a field day with that story because there are so many triggers associated with it. It is just one example.

Interestingly and worth noting, it was determined that the incident was not a crime. We investigated the deaths and determined the cause, but prosecutors declined to pursue the deaths in criminal court. The case made its way through a civil process, and I testified about the investigation. Police work is often that way. Much of it has little to do with crimes, but it is always about people.

There are plenty of dead bodies, and sometimes memories of the ones who are still alive are just as bad or worse. Some of the scenes are beyond description such as bullet holes in people that can be counted by the blood oozing from them; decapitations in motor vehicle accidents; and bodies of infants trapped in cars. We found one dead baby lodged under the front seat of a car long after we had been at the scene. We had no idea the baby was there. There are suicides by shotgun blasts to the head, by carbon monoxide poisoning, by chemical poisoning, by drowning, and by hanging. One man killed himself right in front of me by drinking an organophosphate pesticide. There are the dead bodies that are undiscovered after days or longer in hot homes without air-conditioning that are oozing with maggots. There are bodies with no appearance of trauma that look like they are staring right at you. There are the screams from moms and dads as their kids are burned alive in their bedrooms because a firefighter or cop cannot get to them. There are families torn apart by domestic violence—and the kids who will never be the same. Moreover, there are dead cops. There are cops dead from felonious assaults, cops dead from accidents, and cops dead by their own hand. I have seen every one of these and often multiple times. I say "see," but it is beyond *seeing*. These are experiences that worm their way into the core of the humanness of a cop. They invade every part and remain there forever. These are the tragedies, the likes of which are beyond description, that a cop sees over a twenty-five-or thirty-year career. Most of the time, there is nothing a police officer can do to correct or fix these things. They remain a part of the officer—just like that smell. That is what it is like to be a cop.

Occasionally something good happens, and maybe that is what keeps everybody going. A cop has an interaction with a kid whose world is upside down and is calmed by the officer's presence. A cop finds a lost child. A cop writes a letter of recommendation for a troubled kid that helps get him into the military, and there is pride when the kid returns from basic training as a soldier. There is that family, torn apart by life's events, that a cop helps move onto a better path. There are plenty of good things that happen, but they do not seem to stand out as much. Part of the reason they go unnoticed is because they are just part of the day. It is what the cop does. They are rarely noticed by anyone and particularly not by the cop. Most officers do not embrace and remember the positive things that happen even if they briefly feel good about them. The events that affect us are often bad, and they stay with us.

Robert DeNiro has a great line in the movie *Men of Honor*.[63] He plays the role of Master Chief Billy Sunday and says, "I don't know why anybody would want to be a navy diver." That is a line written for cops because I do not know why anybody wants to be a cop, and I spent more than forty years as one. I am still one in my mind, body, and soul—even if I do not have a badge to prove it. It never goes away.

Policing is long on tradition and family pride, and many officers experienced their finest moments pinning a badge onto the uniform of a son or daughter joining them on the job. Just recently, my academy classmate beamed proudly at his son's acceptance to a state police agency's training academy. Lately, however, we are seeing a new phenomenon. Many officers are no longer excited to learn that their son or daughter is joining the cops. This is very different from the long tradition of a father or mother's pride when a son or daughter went on the job. Many do not want their family members exposed to the dangers and assaults on police. They do not want their sons and daughters exposed to the anger against the police that we see across this country. They do not want them to be frustrated by politicians and the courts. Mostly, I think they do not want them to join them on the job because they do not want them to see what they saw.

My father demonstrated the great lessons of psychological trauma early in my life. I did not learn the lessons then, but I learned them later. My father was a career soldier who was awarded the Combat Infantry Badge, Bronze Star, and Purple Heart during combat in World War II. He also served in Korea during that war. He demonstrated that a good soldier did not talk about what he saw in war or what I would later see and experience in policing. He taught me not to talk about it, not to acknowledge it, and to go about life like it did not happen. My father taught me that the only comfortable place was with those who understood war, and that was with other soldiers.

You might assume that it would be a good thing to be with peers who experienced similar events. It would be good to talk about them and help each other heal. That might be true if it happened, but my father and his veteran family did not talk about them. Later, I would not talk about them either. These were closed stories that were not to be acknowledged or discussed. My father's peers were the soldiers who spent many hours at the Veterans of Foreign Wars (VFW) post across the street from our house. For me, it would be the choir practices, Police Benevolent Association (PBA) meetings, and the Fraternal Order of Police (FOP) hall.

It was called choir practice. It is a phenomenon not unique to the police, but at the same time, it is different for the police. Choir practice is not a few office workers getting together on a Friday at five o'clock to wind down after a long week. It is not a happy hour for office workers, professionals, or even construction workers to have a few drinks, a few laughs, and go home. Choir practice to a police officer is home.

I have experienced many choir practices in my career. It was where I learned that it is normal to go to a bar and drink at seven o'clock in the morning after a midnight shift. It was normal to stay there until noon, go to sleep, and then get up again for the fifth, sixth, or seventh midnight shift in a row. Choir practices occur in all kinds of places, and surprisingly, a bar is not the location of choice unless it is a cop's bar, either owned or controlled. We do not want to be around people who are not like us. Choir practice is a private, safe place for us. We do not want anyone else around. Choir practices occur in parks, rural areas, or station parking lots. Where they occur is irrelevant. What is relevant is their purpose. Their purpose is to provide a place for a cop to go when, in their mind, they have nowhere else to go. At the end of a shift, still operating at a high level of stress, they do not know where else to go. I wish I could say that they only occurred after some traumatic event on the shift, but although that was often true, there did not need to be a tragedy. Choir practice was on after work when there needed to be one. I only understood later in my career what these choir practices were. Critical Incident Stress Management (CISM) and peer support training clarified it for me. The psychologists can explain all of this. I just know what it is because I lived it.

CISM uses the concept that people who experience an event together become part of a homogenous group because of the experience. No one else, other than the people who experienced the event together, is a part of that group. Others are excluded because they did not experience the psychology of it, the physiological changes, or the emotions associated with it. Not everyone experiences these, but some do, and this shared experience helps heal and restore the equilibrium of the group to some kind of normal.

So, for a cop, choir practice was the CISM diffusing that trained peers use to stabilize the effects of a traumatic event. That explains why choir practices are specific to small groups, not open to everyone, and sometimes not even open to other cops. It could be a squad, a district, a precinct, or in a smaller department, it could be multiple squads. The bottom line is that they are about bringing together a homogenous group with the same experiences. There is therapy in the togetherness of choir practice. Most of the time there is little discussion about specific events. It is generally cop talk. Seldom does anyone bare their soul, but if someone occasionally does, everyone usually leaves feeling better or at least numb from alcohol. I have been happier and laughed more in choir practices than at any other time or anywhere else. The self-medicating with alcohol that accompanies these events is a reality, albeit a sad one, of policing. It is our drug of choice because it is legal—and we think we can control it. We may no longer call them choir practice, but trust me, they still occur.

I think you can agree, even if it is begrudgingly, that the police can be affected by the job. Cops are not just witnessing events; they are experiencing and being consumed by them. But why should we care about cops' wellness? I said at the beginning of this book that no one likes a cop, and there is some truth to that. Why should we care how many cops complete the act of suicide and who practiced it long before they did it? Why should we care if they abuse alcohol, have financial problems, become domestic abusers, exhibit poor conduct and behavior, and are disciplined and sometimes fired? Why should we care? They got what was coming to them, right?

We need to care because on the road to self-destruction, they are interacting with the citizenry. They are interacting with people. The cop who creates a national outcry over using unreasonable or excessive force may be a victim himself. He may be a victim of the insidious way the tragedies of policing invade his being. If that sounds like an excuse for a serious problem, let us take a more in-depth look at this.

Why doesn't this happen to all cops? Why don't all cops derail, or as we like to say, "go off the air?" Why does it happen in varying degrees or not at all? Why does one officer involved in a shooting go back to work without any apparent effects—and another officer never returns to duty? These are questions that keep mental health professionals gainfully employed. They cannot be easily answered. They may not be answerable at all.

Even if you do not like cops, can you agree that we do not want them exhibiting poor conduct, using excessive force, or unnecessarily shooting people? If your answer is yes, then what can be done to prevent it? While these unfortunate events cannot always be prevented, is there something that can be done to recognize problems early and mitigate the effects on both officers and the public?

Now more than ever, we hear a lot about mental health and resiliency in the military. The military, specifically former military personnel and the Veteran's Administration (VA), have provided help and support to law enforcement. We know from past wars and today's war on terror that combat, or even the potential for it, can have severe and adverse effects on mental health. Lt. Col. (ret.) David Grossman's excellent books, *On Combat*[64] and *On Killing*,[65] contain information about the personal trauma of combat. He writes a lot about the sights, sounds, and smells associated with the violence of war and how they affect both the physiology and psychology of the person experiencing them.

Many mental health professionals I have spoken with over the years either trained or practiced in veterans' care facilities. Much of what has been learned from the treatment of veterans applies to law enforcement. We know that veterans and officers experiencing the effects of trauma can be helped. We even see the return to full active duty for those diagnosed and living with post-traumatic stress disorder (PTSD). *Diagnosed* is a critical word because the diagnosis of PTSD must be established by a mental health professional. The term gets tossed around frequently and often incorrectly.

The first important thing to accept is that our officers are not impermeable to the experiences surrounding them. We do not issue our officers a nonstick or magic suit, and the effects of a critical incident do not just roll off. Traumatic events can stick and penetrate us. Crisis Support Solutions[66] provides peer support for federal, state, and local organizations. This company defines a critical incident as:

> A situation (or event) that is so powerful, personal and unexpected that it overwhelms and propels those who experience it into a state of crisis. Crisis

is an overwhelmed state of distress that disrupts
(for a time) the way people think, feel and behave.[67]

The definition gives us a little more insight into why people who
experience trauma react differently to it. It helps to explain why that
cop who is involved in a shooting can return to work with little or no
adverse effects—while another cop involved in a similar event never
does. A part of the answer is in the definition itself with the word
personal. These are experiences that are not limited to a specific event
or type of event, that meet a particular criterion, and are personal
and overwhelming. This encompasses a vast range of possibilities
and is difficult to define with any specificity. Maybe Justice Potter
Stewart's statement, "I know it when I see it," is a good analogy.

Resilience—or the term that is often used today, *resiliency*—is
essentially a person's ability to recover from some unfortunate event.
We talk about building resiliency in our officers, but how well are
we doing? I attend the International Association of Chiefs of Police
annual conference just about every year, and I go to as many mental
health and resiliency training sessions as possible. At these sessions,
police department representatives and mental health professionals
talk about resiliency and suggest ways to help officers be more resilient to trauma. There are no silver bullets or specific answers on how
to build resiliency, but there are plenty of examples of departments
where it is working. The single most important and consistent thing
necessary for these programs to be effective is the support of the
chief or executive of that organization. Traumatic events can have
detrimental effects on officers' well-being and—unchecked—can
also cause damage to others. That damage may reveal itself in an
officer's unwanted conduct during citizen interactions and displays
of unreasonable or excessive force. Chief law enforcement officers
must establish mental health and resiliency as a department priority.

Police departments need to embrace the well-being of their
officers in the same manner they approach every other problem in

law enforcement: by coordinating with the necessary people. Police executives need to assemble a team of professionals that represents all of the stakeholders involved. Rank-and-file representation, supervision and management personnel, executives, administration, and mental health professionals are all stakeholders in the commitment to ensure the well-being of officers. A mission statement needs to be developed that acknowledges that officers' exposures to critical incidents can affect their mental health and resilience, and it should clearly state the agency's commitment to address these issues for both officers and the community. Results can be realized only after a police agency's coordinated, committed, mission-oriented demonstration of solidarity.

Mental health professionals need to be carefully selected because they are critical to a police department. This should not be the mental health professional who conducts fitness-for-duty examinations, although they are also essential and should be carefully selected. We should not overlook the preemployment psychological screening of a police applicant or minimize its importance as a hiring tool. Unfortunately, there are times when a police executive needs to know about an officer's continuing fitness for duty and needs a professional determination. The executive needs to have confidence in the person making the determination because discipline and continued employment decisions will be made based, at least in part, on the professional's opinion. Also, mental health professionals doing preemployment and fitness for duty post-employment screenings need to understand what the police executive needs and strive to provide that. Are they assessing whether the officer can go back to work—or is there more to it? For example, can the officer go back to working sex crimes or crimes against children or narcotics? If executives do not identify specific concerns, they may find themselves back in the same situation with that same officer in the future.

A progressive twenty-first-century policing department with a community engagement mind-set and a commitment to fielding highly professional and healthy police officers will go beyond pre-employment screenings and fitness-for-duty exams. Those departments will create mental health and resiliency programs that promote the well-being of their officers. Carefully selected mental health professionals are the core of a department's mental health and resiliency program. That person is working to ensure officers are healthy. The officers' well-being is their priority. They can recognize when officers are not doing well and can help them to be better. They do it by either getting to know the officers directly or through proxies such as trained peer supporters. Trained peer support personnel who operate under the guidance of mental health professionals provide highly effective ways to ensure small issues and small problems remain small. They are noticed early and dealt with before they become management issues.

Employee-assistance programs are almost always available to police officers. These are often viable programs, but they may not be enough to satisfy the needs of a police department that is serious about a wellness program. Police officers must trust the program. If they do not have that trust, they are not going to use it. They are not going to trust that the same program that deals with everyone else in the city, county, or state can deal effectively with cops. That may be misguided. The program may be an excellent one that refers cops to appropriate mental health professionals, but a cop will not get to that referral if she does not trust the program from the beginning. Valid or not, cops want to believe that the mental health professional understands the uniqueness of being a cop. Police departments should research their employee-assistance programs, and the programs should be embraced by all the stakeholders who will be using it.

In some cases, it may be appropriate to have the department's mental health professional be the individual to refer cops who need help to the employee-assistance program. Mental health professionals who gain the trust of the officers can be very helpful in getting them to accept an outside employee-assistance program. In other departments, especially larger ones, it may be appropriate for the department to operate its own employee-assistance program rather than relying on an outside entity to provide officer wellness services. Larger departments with more significant resources have the luxury of doing that with much success. Another option is to proceed on a case-by-case basis under the guidance of the department's mental health professional. Some officers may do well with the employee-assistance program structure as it exists, but others might need an additional referral. The department's mental health professional can be invaluable in these instances.

When I requested funds to go outside of the EPA to get help for an agent-involved shooting, I was fortunate to have the support of the director and a mental health professional working with our CISM team. After that incident, I created a line item in the CISM budget to pay for assistance after these unlikely events. While most officers have health benefits that will pay for mental health services, some officers believe the agency should pay for these services. These are issues that can be handled and resolved by the working group with stakeholder buy-in.

The unnecessary deaths of police officers, especially by suicide, will continue to be a problem until we, as a people, commit to doing everything we can to prevent them. Many are not doing it, and even fewer are saying it. Suicides will still happen, but there can be far fewer if we make this simple commitment. I still recall the police academy definition of a preventable auto accident. It is one in which the driver failed to do everything he reasonably could have done to prevent it. We are not doing everything we can to prevent law enforcement suicides. "Everything we can" means removing the negative stigma that hinders an officer who is experiencing problems from coming forward to talk about them. We need to provide mechanisms through both individual and family education that offer a trusted and effective pathway for wellness. Families are an essential part of that solution because they see an officer like no one else does. If those family members understand and believe in a department's wellness program, they can be crucial to an officer receiving help. We need to remove the blue veil that we all use and shine a very bright light on it to expose it for the illness that it is. Sick people get well with proper treatment, and cops will too. However, they must have confidence in the system that is there to help them.

This does not suggest that we prevent police executives from doing what they need to do in given situations to protect our cops, their families, and our citizens. An officer may need reassignment or may need to be taken off of active duty. Sometimes they will not be able to carry guns. Some officers will never return to policing. However, this can be done professionally with the officer's assurance that the goal is to return him to full-duty status and not to derail his career.

The only way any of this will happen is if all of the stakeholders are committed to it. Some police departments will maintain that it is not workable, it is not affordable, or it is not realistic. It is certainly not easy. However, in our current environment of mistrust, anger, and frustration, the alternative is not acceptable. Without it, police departments will experience ever-increasing behavioral problems and conduct issues, resulting in more internal investigations, public complaints, excessive uses of force, and officers' deaths. Some of these deaths will be by the officer's own hand. Policing is about people, and the police are people.

CHAPTER EIGHT

RECRUITMENT, HIRING, AND TRAINING

We want cops to do a blue-collar job but act like a professional while they are doing it. That is a big request. Sometimes we fall short of accomplishing that lofty goal, but there are some things we can do that will help get us there.

Chapter 8
Recruitment, Hiring, and Training

We can all agree that unreasonable police seizures, although infrequent, are unwanted. However, even one is too many, and this is especially true when it results in death or severe injury. Police are not the only people responsible for injuries and death. Cops are getting hurt and killed too. When this occurs, there are often many contributing factors, and there is no simple solution. Bias can be one factor, but it is not a factor in every unreasonable police action. How do we identify some of these factors, and more importantly, what can we do about them? The first thing we can do is a better job recruiting, hiring, and training police. It sounds simple, but it is not.

Police departments across this country are running out of viable candidates. Many departments are involved in nationwide recruitment efforts to find new cops. This lack of candidates is not new. In the early 1980s, we saw departments sponsoring nationwide recruiting drives. These, however, were efforts to hire experienced cops from states like New Jersey that had very intensive police training programs. New Jersey-trained officers could go to another state, and with minimal indoctrination, go to work without going to the police academy for a full regiment of training. The hiring challenges we see today are different. People are not lining up to join the cops, and many of the ones who do are unable to successfully complete the hiring process. We also need to consider that oftentimes applicants are unsuitable for police work. We may not be doing enough in the recruitment and hiring process to ensure we are putting police officers on the street who can do the job.

Police departments go to trade shows and are on social media and television looking for candidates. The words "no one likes a cop" were never more valid. Police departments want their officers to be representative of the people in the communities they serve, but how can they accomplish this if the people they serve are suspicious and resentful of the police? Young people in those towns are not growing up hearing from friends, family, and peers that joining the cops is a great idea.

I am not going to spend much time writing about testing to qualify to be a police officer, except to say that most departments administer a written examination, a medical screening, and a basic physical fitness test. These are necessary broad-based screening tools because we have to start somewhere. They do not reveal a whole lot except that the applicants who pass them demonstrate that they possess a minimum ability to enter basic police training. I do, however, want to write about what happens next in the hiring process.

Preventing unwanted officer conduct starts in the hiring process. Police agencies need to be committed to hiring the best and the brightest. There is a question that has been hanging around policing since Sir Robert Peel,[68] and that is, "Is policing a job or a profession?" It has been examined, debated, and opined my entire career, and I have never heard a convincing argument for either. Col. Jim Baker's answer, "It depends," is probably the best answer. I think it depends based on the day, time, or event. So, in effect, it is both. We want cops to do a blue-collar job but act like professionals while they are doing it. That is a big request. Sometimes we fall short of accomplishing that lofty goal, but there are some things we can do that will help get us there.

Police need to have the ability and education to understand and apply the law. They must make split-second use-of-force decisions in those tense, uncertain, and rapidly evolving situations. They must continue their educations through both training and formal education and master skills with firearms and intermediate weapons. They must maintain the physical ability and stamina to meet all that the job demands while working shift work, weekends, and holidays. Any definition of a job or profession includes all that a police officer's duties require.

The debate continues on whether cops need to have a college education. The answer again is, "It depends." The officer handling calls for service for an entire career can probably do well without a degree. That officer's sphere of concern is very limited and narrow. His focus is on what is happening right now. The officer is not concerned about budgets, planning, projections, or what might be tomorrow or in the future. That is not to say the officer should not have a degree because everyone can benefit from an education, but the reality is that the uniformed officer handling calls for service needs reality-based, immediate skills. These are learned from field-training programs and experience. They are not theoretical applications to problems. However, the officer who seeks promotions and continues to succeed with more responsibility is going to reach a point where the street experience is not enough of an education to do the job they are expected to do. Many agencies have gradients of educational requirements such as two-year, four-year, and advanced degrees that meet the level of responsibility for the position held. This is probably the best guidance and is consistent with what I have observed of officers both in training and operationally.

Over my career, I have worked with, observed, and trained both college- and noncollege-educated officers from state, local, and federal law enforcement jurisdictions. My personal experience, with all things being equal except education, is that college-educated police candidates or officers demonstrate a greater ability to learn the training material presented. Formally educated people demonstrate a greater application of skills in reality-based scenario training and precisely perform tasks as instructed. After leaving training and during the performance of their duties, I have found that college-educated agents and officers stay closer to the scripts taught in training. However, they do not do as well as their noncollege-educated colleagues when confronted with changes to altering events. These are merely my observations as a trainer, coach, and supervisor and nothing more than that. I cannot overstate the importance of a good field-training officer who can be the bridge between education and performance.

My grandfather got his job because his mother had a local political connection in a neighborhood ward, and for the exchange of a few dollars, his mom secured my grandfather's appointment to the police department. He got a uniform, a badge, and a gun, which he had to purchase himself. I know that because the first thing he did when he retired almost forty years later was sell the only handgun he ever had. Whatever training he may have received was on the job. There was no hiring process designed to elicit his suitability for policing.

Thankfully, our hiring processes are nothing like they were in 1912, but they are not always what they should be either. We already discussed that some agencies are having difficulty finding candidates to become police officers. That is the first problem. Further compounding this is that police executives work hard to ensure their departments are representative of the people they serve. They are not just looking for bodies. Socioeconomic status often contributes to the problem. That is not an excuse for not hiring people who represent their communities. It is a call for police executives to do more and to become more imaginative to figure out ways to find qualified candidates. Many departments do it already through police explorer programs, police athletic leagues, and other similar programs. I recently became aware of an organization similar to scouting but with the mission to develop future public-safety professionals. However, we still have hiring problems, and police think tanks are wondering where they are going to get our next generation of cops.

Education starts early. If a kid grows up in an environment where the people do not like cops, and she models that animosity, there is a good chance we do not have a future police officer in her. However, what if a kid sees injustices and at the same time sees the police as members of the community? What if that kid does not perceive the police as an invading force, and her beliefs are supported at home, in school, in church, and through outreach programs? If we work with community leaders and others to positively engage with kids and their communities, we have a chance. We have opportunities to accomplish the goal of ensuring that policing is about people and not just any people, but the people they serve. There are no simple answers to the recruitment problem, but innovative efforts may be helping.

I serve on the Environmental Crimes Committee for the International Association of Chiefs of Police (IACP). We recently started an initiative designed to identify and recognize people and organizations who contribute to improving environmental factors in their communities. In doing so, we partner with the law enforcement agency where the activity occurred and jointly recognize the person or group for their work. In addition to recognizing the environmental effort, our recognition program provides an opportunity for a law enforcement agency to connect positively with people in its community. We recently coordinated with a police department to recognize local Girl Scout and Brownie troops for their efforts helping other kids impacted by an environmental situation. Maybe a future cop will come out of that group because of it.

Another aspect of the hiring process that can be improved is candidate background investigations. I have conducted many background investigations, and they are not something officers enjoy doing. They are time-consuming, tedious, and require a lot of work. The officer that does the background, however, is critical to ensuring the department is hiring a capable employee. These investigations may reveal unfavorable information such as prior arrests or a poor

driving record. The department needs to determine what prior conduct they are willing to accept to be able to hire people who are
representative of their communities. Sometimes the answer is zero
tolerance, but in other departments, the demonstration of rehabili-
tation or corrective behavior following certain minor offenses may
warrant further investigation. The very obvious driving and criminal
histories are necessary, but more importantly, we look at whether the
applicant candidly reported events. Did the applicant list the speeding ticket he received two years ago or the arrest that showed up on
his record? The agency will weigh these violations or arrests, and they
may not always preclude a candidate's hiring. The agency should be
more concerned if the candidate fails to disclose these events.

A background investigation will often reveal more than answers
to the questions asked. A simple question about marijuana use can
give the investigator information about a candidate's candidness.
A yes answer tells the investigator that this candidate is telling the
truth. A no answer does not reveal as much. Is the candidate telling
the truth—or is he lying because he does not want to tell the investigator he used marijuana? Which officer would you want policing
your neighborhood?

Candidness is the cornerstone of everything a police officer does.
If we are going to have any trust in our police officers, we must be
sure that they are candid when carrying out their duties. Lack of
candidness, or *candor*, is more than lying. A lie results in a charge of
perjury in a judicial proceeding for instance. A lie is a wrong, end
of story. Candor, however, speaks to doing the right thing even if it
falls short of lying. Candor is about the transparency of the truth.
It is about the expectation that our police always tell the truth. We
want them to tell the truth when they act appropriately, and more
importantly, we want them to be truthful when their actions were
inappropriate.

A candidate will usually list references on their application.
It is highly likely that those people will say good things about the

candidate, but not always. They should be contacted, and in-person interviews should be conducted, if possible. I have been surprised by people who were not supportive of the applicant. Vouchers or references are only a starting point, and when possible, investigators should go deeper in their information search. The investigator can identify additional people to talk to from contacts provided by the applicant or can do something as simple as a neighborhood canvas. A neighbor not named in the application may be a great information source.

An applicant's credit history is another important part of an investigation because good money management tends to demonstrate a person who is responsible. When writing new officer evaluations, supervisors have asked me how to evaluate supervisory abilities when the young officer has never supervised anyone. My answer was that they should at least be able to effectively supervise themselves. A credit history is useful in providing the investigator with information about how an applicant supervises or manages his affairs. Poor money management could be a warning sign.

In some agencies, the background investigator does not provide a hiring recommendation. The investigator merely concludes that there was, or was not, anything in the candidate's background that would preclude her from being hired. However, maybe departments should expect more from these investigations. No one in the department, at that time, knows the candidate better. If you have a hiring process that includes diligent background investigators, not merely question askers, then decision-makers should have enough information to analyze candidates. The other point is that many police officers are hesitant to recommend anyone for anything, particularly a law enforcement position. Most of us jealously guard our profession and rarely make recommendations about people. I walked into the chief's office and recommended we hire a guy who ultimately had a very successful career and retired as a State Police major. I also recommended a candidate who had to retire from policing due to post-traumatic stress resulting from a critical incident. Investigators will not always be right, but their opinions can be valuable to police executives making hiring decisions.

Another vital component of police hiring is psychological evaluations, which can help determine if a person is suitable for the job. The test should be relevant to the position sought. All policing is not equal, and because it is not equal, it requires a diverse pool of candidates. A police officer working in a small rural department will have many different challenges than an officer in an urban one. Psychological evaluations give executives some insight into the personality traits of the candidate. These may be indicators, not proof or conclusion, of how that officer will react and handle myriad policing issues. Psychological examinations also provide indicators of a candidate's suitability to be a police officer that do not merely determine fitness. They are not the same thing.

There are plenty of candidates who can be qualified to be officers, but they are not all suitable. Suitability to be a police officer can be the bigger question and the one that causes the problems. The officer who consciously does something contrary to expected conduct or behavioral norms may have had a suitability problem even though he was qualified for the job. The candidate may have unchecked and unlearned biases. Are there indicators that reveal anger issues in domestic situations? Does the candidate have a history of mistreating animals? None of these, in and of themselves, would disqualify a candidate from being an officer, but they contribute to a person's suitability to be one.

I have spoken with mental health professionals about conduct issues that develop in police officers. The question is, did officers with a proclivity for poor conduct demonstrate this before being hired? Were the undesirable traits indicated in the individuals wanting to become officers—or did the officers develop these traits after being exposed to the everyday rigors of the job? Usually, the answer is as expected: "It depends." There are no definitive answers, but we miss finding vitally important information if we do not conduct comprehensive mental health screenings.

Mental health professionals have an essential role in the screening of law enforcement applicants. However, police executives and mental health professionals must have realistic expectations regarding both the usefulness and the limitations of this important resource. They need to take the time to have the necessary conversations to understand the examination results. Too often, police departments—in a hurry to get candidates qualified or hired—bypass this step even when they require psychological testing. They merely accept a written conclusion of a candidate's fitness without understanding the additional useful information revealed in the mental health screening process.

Training is the final piece of the puzzle when determining a candidate's suitability to be a police officer. I cannot overstate the importance of training to prepare officers to act reasonably when they come in contact with people. It begins at the police academy. When the prospective officer shows up at the academy, she has taken both written and oral tests and undergone background investigations and psychological testing. These are sterile environments that do not represent the real-world environment of the street. Basic police training can accomplish this.

Basic police training also filters out candidates who may have the potential for misconduct, poor decision-making ability, poor multitasking ability, and the inability to function in stressful situations. Basic training is especially useful if instructors keenly observe trainees for signs that could indicate unwanted conduct. Even minor issues can become later problems, but they may be correctable in training. Basic training standards should be extremely high. Agencies that do not assess information that relates to a trainee's future demonstrated performance and who are merely looking at test scores are missing the last opportunity to identify a future problem. Union contracts, workplace standards, and even logistics may prevent some agencies from utilizing basic training for this purpose. It is unfortunate because if we are committed to minimizing unwanted conduct and poor decision-making, the most significant opportunity to see it is in basic training.

I am not talking about instructor abuse, hazing, or pointless yelling and screaming, which serve to intimidate rather than teach. I am talking about carefully orchestrated stress during which the student is monitored and evaluated. Occasionally, a certain amount of yelling and screaming may be used as a part of that. A police officer posted on a security line at a demonstration cannot lash out when he is being verbally abused by a demonstrator. He cannot lose his composure or control. He cannot deal with a belligerent drunk who he encounters in a bar the same way he may have when he was a civilian.

Some believe that new hires are there strictly to be trained and that an instructor could inappropriately judge students and ultimately cause them to fail. This could happen. I have seen it. It is wrong, and it must be dealt with when it exists. Nevertheless, the observations and the feedback from an instructor who observes a future police officer continuously for eighteen, twenty, or more weeks is invaluable. At a minimum, instructors' observations should be shared with the department.

Scoring well in the classroom is essential. For example, a student who barely passes report writing in a classroom training environment may have significant problems in a courtroom. Instructional blocks on the Fourth Amendment are among the most important because they lie at the core of all that the police do. It was written to protect the people from the unreasonableness of government, and the police are at the forefront of these government interactions. A police officer who has a command of the ideal of reasonableness, as it was envisioned by the constitutional framers, is less likely to be unreasonable when dealing with people.

Classroom knowledge is only part of the equation. Another

critical factor in police training is the amount of indoctrination officers receive to prepare them to react reasonably in a variety of circumstances. They can answer all the test questions correctly, but that knowledge demonstration is in a sterile environment with an average heart rate, average respiration, and clear vision. There is no fear of interpersonal contact that is causing the prehistoric man to fight, flee, or freeze. Written test questions read in a quiet classroom are easy to answer. Problems on the street in a tense, uncertain, and rapidly evolving environment are different.

We put police trainees and veteran officers in scenarios that are designed to create stress, which forces them to problem solve and multitask just as they need to do on the street. A decision to seize a person either physically or with a bullet cannot wait until the officer rereads *Graham v. Connor* and mulls over the decision. Instead, these decisions are made in tense, uncertain, and rapidly evolving situations. The first time an officer experiences these circumstances cannot be on the street where the stakes are high. We want the first time to be in a training environment where the officer can make mistakes, learn from them, and hopefully not repeat them.

Although trainers cannot replicate real-world scenarios with a stimulus that creates the same level of response as a live event, trainers need to get as close to it as possible. Situational, reality-based training is the most effective way to train our police officers. A good training philosophy is to train the skill, practice the skill, and situationally apply the skill in an environment that is as real as we can get. Together with hiring, training gives us the highest probability that our officers are going to be reasonable in their interactions with people.

Let us take for example a domestic disturbance involving two cohabitants. The first thing I need to train is the law. What is the law governing domestic abuse in my jurisdiction? Do I need to arrest if I see one injured person or two, and what does injury mean? I need to train the officer how to approach and enter the scene of the disturbance safely. I need to teach the officer to recognize highly emotional and volatile situations and the verbal skills necessary to de-escalate the situation. I then need to have officers practice these skills in a controlled environment that is conducive to learning. At this point, we have relatively calm-thinking officers who we can teach and correct. Only after I have developed the officer's skills can I create a simulated reality that approaches, as nearly as possible, what would occur in the real event.

Stress is a tremendous instructional aid for police trainers. There are many ways we introduce stress, including force-on-force training. Boxing and other similar drills are not about who wins. They are about controlling the body's physiological responses to stress so we can think clearly and respond appropriately. It is about not giving up. While it is true that in some physical encounters, it is a fight for life without much rational thought, they are not all like that. The ones that are can be very violent and usually result in an officer's use of force being reasonable. The ones that are not so violent seem to be the ones that get us into trouble. They are the ones that generate excessive and unreasonable force complaints.

As instructors, our goal is to train officers to be safe and while doing so be able to reason under pressure. We strive to create training scenarios that are realistic and demonstrate real-world encounters. Because these encounters can create fear and uncertainty, we try to recreate that level of stress as well. That is difficult to do in a training environment where the realities of danger are simply not there. However, if we use active role players who understand their principal job, we can nevertheless be successful in providing a meaningful training experience. We want our officers to be comfortable on the street, and by handling similar problems in training, we help create confidence in our officers. This confidence enables rational decision-making.

If we are successful in training, we see officers begin to manage physiological responses, which teaches them to react reasonably to situations. The prehistoric man inside him is whispering and telling him that he saw this before, he recognizes it, and he knows what to do. The result is that trained officers do what they need to do while acting reasonably. That is the result we want. When we see that result demonstrated in a realistic training environment, we can expect to see it on the street.

Most of a police officer's day has nothing to do with the use of force or, for that matter, locking up bad guys. Most of the duties of a police officer are civil. The police mediate disputes, solve people problems, and render a wide range of assistance. Even traffic enforcement is mostly civil. In a nutshell, the presence—or the perception of that presence—plays a big part in what the officer does.

Often officers need to do very little. They need to be present, and if they are not present, the fact that they might be is sometimes enough. Why do people generally obey the speed limit? There are far fewer cops than speeders. It is the perception that there might be a cop with a radar unit over the next rise. How many burglaries were prevented by the police car patrolling that neighborhood last night? There is no way of knowing the answers, but a lot of the positive effects of police patrol come from the randomness of it. The patrol need not be seen to suggest that it is there, and it remains a highly effective deterrent to wrongdoing whether it is present or not.

The cops and robbers stuff does happen though, and the dilemma for the use-of-force instructor lies in preparing officers for these infrequent, tense, uncertain, and rapidly evolving encounters. Sometimes they are violent with the potential for serious bodily injury or death to suspects, bystanders, and the police. A police officer does not have the option to retreat from using force and is obligated to use it when necessary to effect a lawful purpose. Police officers must then be trained to not only use force but to use it appropriately and effectively. Appropriate and effective use of force provides the highest potential for minimizing serious injury to both suspects and the police.

There is an adage in tactics training that says, "Speed, surprise, and violence of action is the most effective way to accomplish an objective." That means that when we need to use force, we must be quick. It must be a surprise to the subject we are using it against, and it must be severe enough to accomplish our objective. This creates the highest probability that we can accomplish the objective while minimizing potential risks. We teach officers that when force is necessary, they should quickly use the appropriate amount. It comes down to something that sounds basic, but teaching it so that it becomes learned behavior is another matter.

There are many ways we teach students how to reasonably use force, and the most obvious is skill set training. We teach students, for instance, how to deliver controlled strikes using a baton while minimizing serious injury to the suspect. They are trained to deliver sufficient force to gain control of a suspect. They are not trained to beat a suspect into submission or enact punishment or street justice. Firearms skills training teaches officers to deliver rounds accurately to a threat and to cease firing when the threat no longer exists.

Firearms training and qualifications are not competitive marksmanship tests. The gunfight the officer may someday be engaged in will be highly stressful, and we need to find a way to simulate that on the firing range. We do it with time. We create stress by forcing students to deliver accurate shots in a compressed period. We are not teaching them to shoot fast *per se*. We are teaching them to shoot accurately under stress.

Precision shooting is not taught in police firearms training other than to hone marksmanship skills. Instead, we teach officers to stop a threat quickly. If that threat creates the necessity to use deadly force, it must be used until the threat does not exist. The concept sounds simple enough, but the reality is that training time, ammunition costs, and range availability often prevent officers from being as proficient with firearms as they could be. Indeed, most officers satisfactorily complete a practical examination on the range. This is referred to as "qualification." We develop firearm-handling skills to the point that an officer can demonstrate the minimal level of proficiency established by some governing agency like a state's police officer's standards and training group. The reality is that we are often qualifying them to put holes in a paper target. We are not qualifying them for a deadly force event.

Untrained people often want to know why we do not just shoot someone in the arm or leg to disable them instead of shooting to kill them. There are no lesson plans that teach the police to kill. I will repeat that there is no police firearms training that teaches officers to kill. Firearms instruction teaches the officer to deliver rounds to stop a threat in a tense, uncertain, and rapidly evolving situation. End of story. That means that we teach officers to deliver high-percentage shots to the accessible target area. Usually, that is the center of the observable mass, which equates to the middle torso area of the human body. We do not teach target practice, and some agencies like my own have even gone away from numerical scores on targets. Instead, we look for a score that indicates proficiency and leave it at that. An officer's firearms proficiency is examined using known distance and time constraints. For instance, we can say that 70 or 80 percent of the time, the officer delivered rounds that should incapacitate the threat, and we leave it at that. Whether the officer shot a 100 percent score on that particular day is less important than his or her ability to consistently and proficiently fire the weapon.

We also teach officers a minimum standard of physical or hands-on control skills, but we are not creating MMA[69] athletes in policing. We train officers when to use appropriate, less than deadly force tools such as batons, Tasers, and oleoresin capsicum, or pepper spray as its more commonly known.

Police training, especially the in-service frequency of it, varies across the country. The reality is that agencies with more money and more available time are the ones that train more. Federal agencies like the one I worked for budgeted for use-of-force training and are able to send agents to training without impacting normal operations. Police departments, however, often with strained budgets, cannot afford to train as much as they would like. Ammunition costs alone can be significant. The other problem is that police departments must maintain minimum levels of patrol staffing and often need to pay overtime to send officers to training. The reality is that patrols are staffed first, and everything else comes after that.

There is another training component that is as important as any of the skills described in this chapter. It is critical to an officer's ability to successfully perform in a highly stressful event involving the use of force. This is *mind-set training.* Mind-set training prepares officers to think in a highly stressful and fearful situation. I write a lot about fear in this book because it is a reality for police officers. Yes, folks, cops do get scared. They are people after all. Most people, when confronted with fear, will flee, freeze, or fight. Most people exercise one of these three options even if they do so unconsciously. If they choose to fight and do not have the appropriate skills and training, their fighting will be uncontrolled and for the sole purpose of surviving the encounter. They are acting out of terror.

The police officer only has one option and that is to fight, but that fight cannot be allowed to get out of control. The officer cannot merely fight to survive without any regard for the consequences or the reasonableness of his or her actions. If that were the case, why would an officer fight a hyped-up drug user exhibiting superhuman strength who feels no pain? Instead, the officer would merely shoot the suspect and end the fight. That is what we see so often with the "stand your ground" laws across this country. We cannot do that because of those fifty-four words I wrote about in another chapter of this book. Our actions must be reasonable.

Warrior and *sheepdog* are just a couple of the many terms that are a part of police culture. We taught them as mind-set philosophies for law enforcement officers. We followed great inspirational speakers like Lieutenant Colonel David Grossman and his "warrior mind-set" philosophies.[70] The pages of my copies of his *On Combat*[71] and *On Killing*[72] are dog-eared and filled with notes. I used his, and many other great works, in my use-of-force lectures.

Good use-of-force instructors will use whatever methodology they can to prepare officers for that use-of-force encounter. Mindset training is an excellent place to start. Instructors impress upon officers that police use of force is not a game. There is a great line by Frank Overton's character, General Bogan, in the 1964 movie, *Fail Safe*.[73] During a tense, cold war scene, strategic air command post staff are watching the plotting board as Soviet and American aircraft kill each other. The staff begins to cheer and applaud, and Overton's character sternly announces, "This is not a football game."[74] The tactical skills we teach are not for playing video games or paintball. We are teaching officers to be prepared to use force because someone's life, not a game score, may depend on it. We do not award trophies for police uses of force. We use concepts like visualization, which has been around for a long time and practiced by professional athletes. For example, the wide receiver who visually sees the ball coming into his hands and the batter who visualizes seeing the ball as he swings the bat and makes contact. Good use-of-force instructors teach these concepts to officers. Officers are encouraged to practice this visualization technique to prepare them for conducting car and pedestrian stops and field interviews and for use-of-force events. Thinking about what people are going to do can prepare them for what they will do.

My first bank robbery in progress was a blur because I did not know what to do. I was the first car on the scene, and where to position my vehicle and how to direct other responding units was entirely foreign to me. I can still hear the words of Sgt. Michael O'Donnell telling me on the radio that if the robbers come out, they do not go back in. I did not even know what he meant. Did that mean that I was supposed to shoot them? Sgt. O'Donnell would later explain that allowing the robbers to reenter the bank would enable them to hold employees hostage, creating the potential for additional casualties. Thankfully, as it turned out, they made their getaway before I got there. After that, I never responded to an armed robbery without knowing what to do. After that first experience, I thought about what I would do in the future. I ran through my mind responses, approaches, and what I would do if I confronted the robbers. I practiced visualizing what I would do at the next robbery. I was practicing visualization, although I did not know it at the time. We know visualization works, and we teach it because it works.

We also teach word association concepts such as Grossman's lamb, sheepdog, and wolf concepts.[75] To most people, a lamb is a vulnerable animal. We associate a lamb with nursery rhymes and Bible stories. A lamb stays close to the rest of the flock for protection, runs from danger, has a fluffy wool coat, and is generally a very passive animal. Grossman uses the analogy that most people are like lambs. They fear confrontation and interpersonal aggressiveness, and they run from danger. People, for the most part, are nonaggressive or passive, friendly, and generally very peaceful.

Sheepdogs, in most folklore, children's books, and nursery rhymes are the protectors of the sheep herd. The sheepdog is constantly vigilant, is looking for threats, is usually big and strong, is friendly to the sheep, and is nonaggressive unless necessary to protect the sheep. The sheepdog is analogous to the police officer. The characteristics demonstrated by the vigilant and kind sheepdog protector is what we want our officers to be. Also like the sheepdog, we want our officers to be able to deliver force when necessary.

The wolf, however, is another matter. The wolf is a predator, is sneaky, and is capable of serious violence or death. The wolf steals food from other animals and is powerful and aggressive. Generally, the wolf produces fear in most of us. The big bad wolf will blow your house down according to the story. We must protect the sheep from the wolf's assaults. The wolf is analogous to the bad guys who want to do people harm, disrupt their ways of life, and assault and rob them. The wolf must be dealt with swiftly and effectively.

With this in their mind-set for the lecture, we set the stage. The sheep or people or citizens require protection from the wolf or bad guys. The protector must be the sheepdog or police officer. We teach the officer to think about the characteristics of the sheepdog and emulate them in their daily comings and goings. This fundamental set of analogies is used to get officers thinking about mind-set.

There are all kinds of analogies including one using the colors red, yellow, and green. Green is analogous with how most people go about their lives. They move along on a green light without a care in the world. They go from the store to the parking lot without looking around for that attacker who may be approaching. They only pay attention to what they are doing—not to what is going on around them. Mostly, they are oblivious to their surroundings. Yellow is where we tell our cops to be. Yellows go about their business with a certain amount of caution that varies depending on the circumstances. In yellow, we teach them to be prepared for the unexpected, to be ready for whatever may happen, and to react appropriately to events. To be yellow is to be vigilant, cautious, and prepared. I would often tell officers to take a lesson from the firefighter who goes into an unfamiliar area. Watch that firefighter scan the room and identify exits, fire alarms, and suppression systems. The police can learn a lesson about situational awareness from the fire service. Red is action. When we are in red, we are reacting to the event we detected in condition yellow. We are moving to solve a problem or neutralize a threat. Some teaching aids go a step further, using the color black as an action phase and dropping the red back to something just short of that. The colors are meaningless. What is meaningful is that officers understand that we want them in a state of mental preparedness. We want them paying attention.

These analogies seem to be acceptable to most people and do not generate a lot of disagreement. Lambs and sheep do not cause anyone concern. However, some analogies are generating a lot of opinions and opposing views. *Warrior* leaves the typical image of a police

55555555555

officer behind and develops into images of special operations personnel, ninjas, or soldiers. On the other hand, Kevin Costner's character of a United States Coast Guard rescue swimmer in *The Guardian*[76] may be a good example of what we want our police officers to be.

Much of what I wrote in this chapter sounds like simple words on the pages of a book, but on the street, things are different. The realities of the street where that officer works can derail even the best training. It can be an uncontrollable reality that contributes to chaotic situations that are not easy to rationally solve. Sometimes the rational has gone out of these situations, and they are barely manageable. They are not laboratory scenarios with limiting factors. They are dangerous encounters with limitless possibilities for injury or death. Even the most highly qualified and best-trained officers can act unreasonably in a given situation. People react differently to different stimuli at different times. It is complicated.

Special Agent Elliot Ness, played by Kevin Costner, uses deadly force in the movie *The Untouchables*.[77] He is told by Sean Connery's character, Officer Jim Malone, that he did his duty and should go home and sleep well. Going home safe was the mantra we all taught our law enforcement students. If we went home safe, it was a successful day. That has not changed and should still be our absolute number one priority. However, I recently read an interview with a young cop who works the streets in an urban city. He had a slightly different take on the old mantra. He said that we used to teach our cops that the only thing that mattered was to go home safe, but that is no longer enough. He said that now we want everyone to go home safe, including the victim, the suspect, and the officer. Anyone who feels that this is contradictory to our age-old mantra needs to rethink it. The old mantra has not changed at all. It is still our number one priority. We merely added people to it. We are saying it because we want to be better. The officer who follows the modified mantra is the kind of person we want wearing a badge and carrying a gun in our communities. We want the officer who recognizes that everyone's life matters and that any life lost, no matter how necessary, is a tragedy. We are in the business of preventing tragedy.

Some people believe that we have police officers on the street who should not be there. They believe that these are the officers who are using excessive force, are biased, and are not in compliance with the rule of law. If that is true, and we may have a few, how do we change it? How do we get better officers? We are only going to get them if the people in our communities supply them. We want the best and brightest, and we cannot be content to take what we can get. To do that, we need to start in our communities and not at job fairs. By that time, it can be too late. When we talk about community engagement, we need to expand our mission to include developing future police officers. Future police officers are in our communities right now because that is where the people are, and the police are the people.

The greatest hope for improving our police departments and creating better police officers lies in recruitment, hiring, and training. They are the foundation of law enforcement, and the survivability of our profession depends on them.

CHAPTER NINE

SMART POLICING

Sometimes we can slow things down and get time on our side. It is not about not doing our job. It is not about ego. It is about being smart. Either we get smarter on our own, or the courts and our government will force it on us.

Chapter 9
Smart Policing

I wrote a lot about fear factors and a subject's actions that create stimuli that influence an officer's reactions. However, what happens when the police contribute to things getting out of control? We do not like to admit that we can be a part of the problem. We prefer to say that the suspect is the one responsible for the force used. In other words, if the suspect had complied with police commands, the police would not have needed to resort to the level of force used. I agree with that under most circumstances, but with today's policing, the analysis goes deeper.

There is a long-standing teaching point in police use-of-force training, which is that the subject engaged by the police is responsible for what happens to himself or herself. If a subject does not comply with police direction and the situation becomes physical, it was a result of the subject's noncompliance. If a subject is holding a knife or gun, or the officer reasonably believes she is, and she does not comply with police commands and is shot or even killed, she created the situation that resulted in the police use of force. The Court told us that we need to evaluate police use of force at the moment it is used without the benefit of hindsight or foresight of what might occur in the future. If the subject complied, the officer would not have used the force that he did. The subject is responsible for what occurred.

That teaching point remains valid and is accurate as far as it goes. Let us examine a police-initiated stop and put aside for a moment the reasonableness of the seizure. We will get back to that. The person at the focus of the stop has her hands in her jacket pockets and will not show them to the officer as requested. Tensions rise as the officer continues to issue verbal commands, and the subject continues her noncompliance. In the absence of other factors, the officer has essentially two choices. One is to terminate the stop and say, "Have a nice day ma'am." The other choice is to initiate some level of force to safely ensure the subject is not hiding a weapon in her pockets. We do not routinely teach cops to walk away from situations, especially those they initiated. If the subject remains noncompliant or resists, the officer will use physical, mechanical, or even deadly force to overcome that resistance. The officer will most likely charge the subject with resisting arrest and possibly assault on a police officer. Most police officers would conclude that the officer acted reasonably because if the subject had complied with the officer's commands, the use of force would not have occurred. The subject created the necessity for the police to use force.

However, the subject, along with others, may see the situation differently. They may argue that the officer had no reason to stop the subject. They may also argue that the officer had no right to search the subject or use physical force. They may go even further and believe that the resisting arrest and assault charges were made in an attempt to cover up the illegal actions of the police. The same incident is viewed differently by different people. We can be very far apart from any common ground regarding our views of the reasonableness of this police action.

What if more information was available about why the police initiated the stop in the first place? Opinions about the reasonableness of it may change. If the police stop a subject suspected of committing violent crimes, is a drug dealer, or is otherwise dangerous to the public, many citizens would agree in the legitimacy of the police action. These kinds of police engagements are much more acceptable to people, but these incidents are not routinely the ones that create the controversy, public outcry, and anger directed at the police. Most citizens, whether they like the police or not, want the dangerous bad guys off the street. Even if we do not always agree on the police methods, we tend to have more tolerance for police actions when a dangerous individual is preying on innocent people.

However, sometimes these situations are fluid, and they ebb and flow as the events unfold. A violent offender who is contained by the police may have been shot and killed. The public may have other opinions as to how the police should have handled the situation. Why couldn't they wait him out, use tear gas, or some other method? Why did they have to shoot him? Some excessive force allegations are based, at least in part, on the assertion that the police had no lawful reason to do whatever it was they were doing. Often people allege that the initial police actions to stop or detain the subject were improper, and thus the resulting application of force was unreasonable. They assert that the police are routinely violating people's rights by these illegal actions, and they lack the justification or authority to do much of what they are doing.

The stop-and-frisk procedure, which has mostly disappeared from police practices, led to allegations of unlawful police actions. Stop and frisk was a proactive police procedure designed to reduce violent crime. It accomplished that by identifying offenders who were carrying guns and narcotics. It was met with opposition from citizens who alleged that the police were using race and skin color to stop citizens who were not violating any laws. They alleged the police were illegally stopping people and conducting illegal searches. If police discovered contraband, such as narcotics or firearms, people were arrested, and sometimes these arrests resulted in incarceration. People alleged that this was all the result of police misconduct. During these events, suspects failed to comply with police commands because they believed the police were acting unlawfully or beyond the scope of their authority. That failure to comply likely resulted in officers using force to gain compliance, and if met with resistance, the force used was escalated. This resulted in allegations of police misconduct, including racial profiling and excessive uses of force.

Many police departments now prohibit officers from the procedure known as stop and frisk. Community citizen complaints and allegations of racially motivated stops and illegal searches forced cities to evaluate the costs versus the benefits of the procedure. Stop and frisk was effective for seizing illegal firearms and narcotics and arguably made an impact on the number of street crimes in the areas where it was utilized. However, the citizen complaints and substantiated cases of police exceeding their authority ensured its demise.

Stop-and-frisk actions aside, investigative stops are an integral part of policing. The police would not be able to do their jobs if they were not able to investigate citizen reports of illegal activity. Routine police observations would be useless if they were not able to investigative them. That old police admonition, "Observation without investigation is of little or no value," is as valid today as it was when I first heard it more than forty years ago.

Recall for a moment that interference of a person by the government must be reasonable. The Fourth Amendment assures citizens that their freedoms cannot be unreasonably infringed upon by the government. Most of the time, an infringement of that freedom, lawful or not, is going to be by the police. The key word is *reasonable*. All investigative stops are not illegal or unpermitted. Only the unreasonable ones are. I write about reasonableness in every chapter of this book, but what is it exactly? The answer is, "It depends." How can police actions be reasonable and stay within the confines of the rights guaranteed by the Constitution? The Court gave us some guidance.

Terry v. Ohio was a case decided by the Court in 1967. Since then it has been used as the basis to determine the reasonableness of all investigative stops. This case stands as the Fourth Amendment standard. Cleveland Police Detective McFadden was working a familiar downtown area of retail establishments. He observed two men on a street corner who were walking past a store and looking into the windows. They walked past a particular store several times and then returned to the corner and had a brief conversation. This occurred at least twenty-four times. A third man approached the two at some point, had a brief conversation with them, and walked away. Detective McFadden suspected the two were preparing to rob the store, and he moved toward them. The two men began to walk away, and the third man joined after a short distance. McFadden caught up to the three subjects and asked one of the subjects for his name. The subject mumbled something inaudible, and at that point, McFadden spun the subject around and physically controlled him. McFadden conducted a pat down of the subject's outer clothing and came upon an object which he recognized, by feeling it, as a handgun in the subject's coat pocket. He attempted to remove the firearm from the coat pocket but was unable to because of the object's position in the pocket. McFadden moved all three subjects into a store and recovered the firearm. He continued his frisk of the other two subjects and located one additional firearm on a second subject. McFadden charged the subjects with illegal possession of a firearm. The issue that arose was whether the search was reasonable. If the search was not reasonable, the guns could not be used as evidence against the subjects. The guns were the only evidence of a crime McFadden had. The Court had long determined that if police conduct was unreasonable, any evidence uncovered as a result of that conduct would be inadmissible in a prosecution. This is known as "the exclusionary rule," which was named as such because it excludes improperly obtained evidence.

The Court in *Terry v. Ohio* would define the reasonableness of an investigative stop, which is quite possibly the most routine of all police activity. At issue in *Terry* was whether or not the seizure of the handguns was the result of an unreasonable search and based upon an unreasonable stop. The police may only search if: (1) they have an order or warrant from a court to do so; (2) they have probable cause to believe that a crime has been committed and the area they want to search contains evidence of that crime; and (3) the search is of an arrested person including areas accessible to him or her.

McFadden, however, had none of these scenarios. He had no search warrant. He had no information that a crime had been committed, and he had not arrested any of the three subjects for any crime. At the point that he found the gun, he was merely detaining them. They were not arrested. However, McFadden did have, based upon his years of policing this area, a reasonable suspicion that criminal activity was occurring.

Reasonable suspicion is more than a guess or a hunch, but it is not the probable cause that would have enabled McFadden to conduct a search or make an arrest. Specifically, these men were demonstrating actions that McFadden reasonably suspected were consistent with someone casing, or preparing to rob, a store. McFadden also knew that armed offenders often committed these types of robberies. McFadden was obeying his basic police training by investigating what he observed. In doing so, he conducted what we now know is a frisk for weapons that could harm him or bystanders.

The Court explained that a simple frisk is less than a search and was demonstrated by McFadden as he patted down the outer clothing. McFadden did not go inside the clothing to search but instead patted the outer clothing. It was during this limited intrusion of a pat down that McFadden encountered what he immediately recognized as a firearm. The Court determined that McFadden reasonably suspected criminal activity was occurring, or was about to occur, and that it was reasonable for him to approach and stop the three men suspected of that activity. It was further reasonable for McFadden to perform a frisk for his and other's safety because armed offenders typically commit the type of crimes he was investigating. McFadden immediately recognized a handgun during the lawful frisk and thus was legally able to seize the firearm and arrest the subject in possession of it.

The police learned some critical lessons from the *Terry v. Ohio* decision that became, and continue to be, standard police practices. The first is that when the police have a reasonable suspicion that criminal activity has or is about to occur, they may make an investigative stop of a person in order to investigate that activity further. Second, if a reasonable suspicion exists that the investigation may involve criminal activity in which weapons are reasonably expected to be present, they may conduct a frisk for those weapons to ensure their safety and the safety of others. Weapons discovered may be seized and used in the prosecution of the offender.

The police could not effectively conduct operations without the *Terry v. Ohio* standard because it allows them to conduct an investigation pursuant to an observation. *Terry v. Ohio*, however, did not give the police open-ended investigative stop authority. It also did not give the police the authority to automatically frisk every person who was the focus of an investigative stop. The Court instead told us that an officer's observations together with circumstances about the stop are factors to consider in determining a reasonable suspicion that weapons may be present. The Court told us that our information need not meet the probable cause standard, but it needed to be more than a hunch in order to have the authority to investigative further.

It is easy to become overly aggressive with what we have come to call a *Terry* frisk, partly because of the Court's deliberate vagueness in describing it. We sometimes hear officers explain that they are conducting a *Terry* frisk for officer safety, which is only partly true. While it is true that they are doing it for officer safety, the reasonableness in doing it requires further refining. The frisk for weapons that the Court described in *Terry* requires a little more than an officer safety conclusion. *Terry* also requires police to have a reasonable suspicion that weapons may be present. While providing the police wide latitude in defining reasonable suspicion of the presence a weapon for the safety of the officers and others, it does not provide a blanket authorization to frisk anyone with whom police come in contact.

The investigative stop guidance that arose from the *Terry v. Ohio* decision has been around since 1967, and we still train cops in how to conduct investigative stops that are consistent with it. Most of us even refer to an investigative stop as a *Terry* stop or a *Terry* frisk. What then is the difference between the procedure we know as "stop and frisk" and a *Terry* stop? They appear to be the same. They appear the same because they are both investigative stops. *Terry*, however, set forth particular parameters within which police can conduct a stop and frisk for weapons. Stop and frisk is more analogous to a consent search in which a subject grants consent. The premise for stop and frisk is that the police can approach anyone in a public place and ask to speak with him or her. The person can say, "Yes," and engage with the officer, or the person can say, "No." If the subject talks to the officer, the officer is going to be listening and watching for clues. These are clues that could suggest that the person is involved in criminal activity. If the officer develops a reasonable suspicion of criminal activity that could involve weapons, the officer can reasonably conduct a frisk.

Officers can also, without probable cause or even reasonable suspicion, ask a person for permission to search his or her bag or case. It is all permissible because the police are not infringing upon anyone's right to be secure in their persons and possessions from unreasonable searches and seizures. There is no intrusion without permission.

The America we live in requires us to be diligent in ensuring weapons are not brought into entertainment venues, sporting arenas, and certain public buildings. Usually, a private security firm will handle these searches of bags and sometimes people. The police may also be present as a part of an assignment or detail. These are considered consent searches since the person is agreeing to it because it is a requirement for entering the venue. Event tickets and signs posted outside venues inform patrons that they are subject to a search and will be denied entry if they do not consent to it.

My wife and I were returning from Italy last summer and arrived at the Rome airport for our departing flight. We were met at the ticket counter by a pleasant ticket agent who engaged us in conversation. She asked us where we traveled during our trip, and she went on to ask more questions that were not merely routine questions about our trip. We thanked her and went on our way. My wife remarked at how pleasant the agent was and how nice it was for her to be so interested in our trip. I joked with her that we had just been stopped and frisked. The truth is that it was not a joke at all. The ticket agent purposely engaged us in that conversation. Since everything we told her seemed to make sense and was reasonable, we did not rouse her suspicions. However, if she had concerns about anything we said, she would have investigated us further or notified law enforcement.

The problem with stop and frisk, as I described earlier in this chapter, is the allegations that were being made about it. What factored into the officer's decision to initiate the stop and frisk, and how credible were the officer's assertions about the stop? Also, some people are intimidated by police officers and would not be comfortable refusing the officer's engagement. Stop and frisk was not bad—quite the contrary. It was highly effective in proactive policing and resulted in seizures of guns, narcotics, and dangerous persons. However, it was easier for cities and departments to prohibit stop and frisk and avoid the controversies that accompanied it. Investigative stops though, pursuant to *Terry v. Ohio*, are alive and well and are an important investigative police tool.

Investigative stops are an essential tool for law enforcement for all the reasons I have indicated. They enable an officer to move from mere observation to developing facts about an event in question. Investigative stops, in and of themselves, are minimally intrusive,

but when the police use force, they can become the basis for misconduct allegations. This can be especially true when the police do not
uncover illegal activity as a result of the stop. Moreover, in some of
these instances, a person is charged with assaulting a police officer
or resisting arrest without a charge for whatever predicated the stop.
These can become especially difficult for a prosecutor.

For example, an officer initiates an investigative stop because he
has a reasonable suspicion of illegal activity. Taking it a step further,
the officer reasonably suspects that the activity typically involves
firearms. The officer stops the individual and conducts a pat down
of the subject to ensure there are no weapons present. If the subject
resists, the officer will likely use force to detain the subject. The
officer uses force, which escalates as the subject continues to resist
the officer. We can see where this is going, and it is not going to end
up well for anyone—the subject *or* the officer. An incident like this
can result in the subject being charged with both resisting arrest and
assaulting the officer even though the original reason for the stop
may not have resulted in any charges.

It is easy for people to write about possible solutions to police
excessive use-of-force encounters. The simple solution they offer is for
everyone to comply with the officer's commands. Compliance will
almost certainly reduce police use of force. I would agree that it may
avoid some of these problems, but I do not agree that it is the solution.
The United States of America is not a police state. That means that
the government cannot regulate the lawful conduct of its citizens and
can only interdict conduct when it is unlawful. Some of the people
who are the focus of these investigative stops are concealing criminal
activities. They know the police will arrest them if they are carrying
a firearm or narcotics, and they will do whatever they can to avoid it.

However, people who are going about their daily business and
are not involved in criminal activity resent being stopped by the
police. They both resent it and, for any number of reasons, do not
believe they need to comply with police authority. They believe the

officer is not acting lawfully and is exceeding her authority. They are suspicious of the police, challenge their lawful authority, and will not comply with direction or commands. When these suspicions combine with real or perceived years or decades of wrongs by the government against a race, gender, or culture, the problem can be very acute and severe. The suspicions become beliefs.

The fact is that disregarding or failing to comply with an officer's commands can have serious consequences for both the subject and the police officer. A police officer's decision to initiate a citizen contact usually includes at least an unconscious decision to see that contact through to its logical conclusion. We teach it that way in our scenario-based training. If the person believes that the police are exceeding their lawful authority, he may decide to resist the contact in some manner. Often it is verbal, but it may escalate to physical as well. The police officer has essentially two choices. One is to disengage from the contact and terminate it. The other is to continue it until she is satisfied that criminal activity is not occurring—or she arrests the subject. Unfortunately, it is during this determining phase that the problem occurs. Rarely is a police officer going to disengage from a contact without satisfying the reason for it.

A person was recently observed making statements on social media that could appear threatening to the president of the United States. The statements were viewed that way by the Secret Service, and officers went to the subject's home to investigate. The woman who was the subject of the allegation allowed two officers into her home to speak with her as another family member recorded the event. She maintained she had a right to speak freely and that the officers had no authority to question her. She refused to talk to them about the social media post and asked them to leave. The officers had two choices. They chose to leave. If they chose the other option, they would have continued to pursue the matter by either detaining or further questioning her. The latter decision would have likely met with resistance and an escalation of force.

Subjects encountered by the police that play a part in the escalation can conversely help to avoid the escalation. People confronted by
the police either believe that confrontation to be lawful and within
police authority, or they do not. Regardless, they must comply with
the officer's instructions. There is no other reasonable option for a
person who is the subject of police contact. That reality is not popular, especially among people who believe they have tolerated police
wrongs for a long time. However, we cannot debate the lawfulness
of police contact on the street. The place to debate the lawfulness
of a police encounter is not when and where it is happening. This is
not justifying or condoning inappropriate police conduct. It is the
only option if we want to reduce police uses of force that result in
injuries and death.

There are numerous avenues for a person to challenge the reasonableness of police action or seek remedy for excessive force. The
reasonableness of a police encounter must be determined by a com-
petent authority, which includes agency internal affairs units and
the courts. Any person who believes actions by the police were
unreasonable should pursue their allegations through those various
avenues. Police internal affairs, the office of professional standards,
and program integrity units all exist to ensure that a high level of
integrity and professionalism exists in the agency. They investigate
allegations of misconduct and present the results of those investigations to police executives. Police executives can, and often do, take
administrative action to both correct and punish an officer's conduct
when warranted. If the behavior rises to the level of a criminal act,
they will refer the matter to the appropriate criminal investigative
agency, such as the prosecutor or attorney general. These allegations,
whether substantiated or not, can provide a mechanism and be the
vehicle for changes in police operations. Challenges to police actions
in a court of law can determine their legitimacy and provide remedies to a wronged subject. These remedies could include suppressing

evidence obtained from an unreasonable action and both civil and criminal sanctions against the officer or police department.

These options sound like the typical police response, and they are often met with disbelief that justice will prevail for people wronged by the police. The investigative process may not seem fair, and it does not help the subject at the time the police encounter is occurring. However, as I indicated, the lawfulness of police actions cannot be debated on the street. We see the results of that too often. We see people severely injured or killed.

Some people believe that the police cover for their own and that generally it is a waste of time to bring these actions. However, the severity of the remedies demonstrates the seriousness in which we view Fourth Amendment violations. Suppression of evidence results in its inadmissibility in a trial regardless of its importance to the prosecution. Civil and criminal sanctions against the officer can result in loss of his job and his pension and incarceration. The police agency and its government can be held responsible to pay significant compensatory and punitive damages. So even though the Court has provided much latitude to the police regarding Fourth Amendment intrusions, it also has established very severe penalties for violations.

Some people, especially those championing police-reform causes, may say that the remedies, although welcome, are not enough. Some believe that more needs to be done to prevent these violations from occurring in the first place. The police are doing more, but we are not there yet. In reality, we may never be because of the complexities of each use-of-force situation. Those tense, rapidly evolving, and uncertain events do not allow time for a police officer to know everything that is occurring. They are dealing with situations that— in their trained minds—require the actions they are taking. These are high-stress situations with the potential for someone, often the subject, to be seriously injured or killed. It happens more often than any police executive wants it to, and even one event is too many.

Even one unreasonable intrusion upon the rights of the people of the United States is too many.

We see law enforcement executives across this country accepting responsibility for the inappropriate actions of their officers when they occur, and we see them demonstrating corrective actions to prevent a reoccurrence. That is what we want to hear from police leadership and what we want to see occurring in departments. It is that kind of leadership that builds trust between the police and the people. Trust is really what this is all about. If we trust officers to do the right thing and address instances when they do not, we can begin to trust that they will do the right thing all of the time.

So that is the real problem. We are finally getting to it. It is not merely the unreasonableness of the police action. The real problem is mistrust of the police. The mistrust that leads people to believe that the police will not thoroughly investigate allegations of misconduct and the courts will always side with the police. Mistrust is not going to allow any reasonable person to believe they are going to get a fair deal from anyone. Mistrust reinforces what people have seen over and over again throughout their lives. Some of these are perceived, and some are real, but it does not matter. The perception is not a perception to them. It is a reality.

This sounds an awful lot like that cynical cop I wrote about in another chapter. The cop who has been lied to, who regularly sees the same unfair circumstances unfold, and who generally mistrusts everyone around him, including the agency he works for, the courts, and the people he serves. Wait a minute. Both the people and the police are experiencing similar cynicism. That does not sound right. Aren't the police on one side and the people on the other? Isn't it especially true when the police shoot a young brown or black man who did not have a gun? Blue lives matter. Black lives matter. Both have strong opinions about what occurred. The police view what they did as reasonable, and the people cannot see how it could be.

The fact is the police are the people, and the people are the police. They are experiencing the same mistrust, frustration, fear, anger, and division. We can build trust, lower frustration, lessen fear, temper anger, and join and not divide. But not during a use-of-force incident. We cannot talk about it then. It is not open for debate during those situations.

We talked about complying with police commands as one way of reducing police uses of force. My hope is that we can agree on how critical it is to minimize an escalation of force even if we do not agree with it. Even if we think it is something a person should not have to do. Another thing that needs to happen is that the police must demonstrate a willingness, and even more than that a determination, to do the right thing. That starts with statements like the one made by Chief Dekmar from LaGrange, Georgia, to the citizens of his city. It starts with chiefs of police building community trust through civic groups, churches, schools, and numerous other venues that provide life to a community. It starts with a chief who will not leave a stone unturned to build trust in his or her community. The people of that community want to live a peaceful life, free to pursue their desired quality of life without unreasonable intrusions by predators, violence, and the police. The people of that community want to trust and build partnerships with their police because they both want the same things. The police are the people, and the people are the police.

This police and community trust did not exist in Ferguson, Missouri, so it is not a wonder why the shooting of Michael Brown by Officer Darren Wilson resulted in the tragedy it did. Community engagement and trust must be a goal of any police department. Challenges that will come cannot deter an agency from accomplishing this goal and maintaining it as well. The people need to acknowledge these engagement initiatives by the police and be willing to evaluate, and hopefully accept, the legitimacy of the department's efforts.

The police, on the other hand, need to police smarter. What does that mean—and how do they do it while adhering to their oath to protect and serve? To police smarter, cops can exhibit more control in situations that can quickly escalate. Cops reading this are likely thinking that I am being unfair. They are correctly thinking that they cannot predict whether that subject is going to attack them, which will require them to use force. I agree up to a point. However, the research about felonious assaults on police officers tells us that often there are signs of an impending attack. We teach pre-assault indicators in almost every use-of-force training. We teach officers to look for the signs. Our officers are not necessarily missing the signs or disregarding them, but they are not always heeding their warnings either. Also, there are times that officers can choose a better option or course of action. Sometimes, officers can orchestrate the contact or stack the deck in their favor.

Do we need to initiate a pedestrian or car stop without another unit or when we are in a dark, desolate area, or can we wait until we have some safeguards in place? Can we make that stop after we place ourselves in a position of advantage? Can we stay with the focus of the stop until we get additional units or are in a more suitable area to make the stop? I can avoid hanging out of the window of a car and being dragged down the highway if I do not reach into the car in the first place.

I have been teaching cops for a long time, and I know that we need to police smarter. There are far too many police encounters that escalate into unnecessary, untenable situations that result in cops getting hurt and being the subjects of internal investigations, resulting in discipline or criminal convictions and jail. These encounters result in the deaths of subjects who, although may have committed a crime, should not be dead because of it. I am not suggesting that the police should not be proactive, that they should disregard responsibilities, or not police at all. I am suggesting that they do all of this smarter. Many officers will oppose what I am saying because they believe that proactive policing makes a difference, helps keep our streets safer, and is necessary to keep them safe while they do their jobs. I could not agree more, but I am suggesting that they be smarter about it. There is also an inherent amount of ego and misplaced bravery in play in what the police do. Cops do not need to prove anything.

There is plenty of rhetoric about the police deciding that enough is enough and deciding to give up on proactive policing. If cops move from proactively doing their jobs to merely answering calls for service, the streets will not be safe, and the crime rate will escalate. We have seen slowdowns too. We have seen lower arrest numbers, lower ticket numbers, blue outs, and various demonstrations resulting from job frustration over the years. However, I also know cops need to vent their frustration and will do that in a variety of ways. I also know that they will not give up policing. They will proactively police and will do what they joined up to do. Our cops are better than that.

Michael Brown is dead. Darren Wilson's life will never be the same again. Neither of these things should have happened. The grand jury, a pool of the people, said that Darren Wilson's actions were reasonable when he shot Michael Brown. Darren Wilson was exonerated of Michael Brown's death by the grand jury, the district attorney, and the Department of Justice. Why then did we see the violent citizen protests against police and government that occurred as a result? The reasons, at least in part, are rooted in police mistrust, especially those that existed in Ferguson, Missouri, when the incident occurred. They are also attributable to the many strong beliefs that Darren Wilson's reactions were inappropriate responses to Michael Brown's actions. These beliefs, real or perceived, are firmly grounded in what some of Ferguson's citizens personally experienced over time with the police. They believe the actions of the police resulted in Brown's death and not the other way around. Taking it a step further, to some people, what happened to Michael Brown was indicative of many unchecked police actions in America. These may be perceptions, but to many people, they are reality.

I am not going to introduce my personal opinion about what

happened on August 9, 2014, in Ferguson, Missouri. The investigation is closed. Some would argue that the case investigation was thorough, and others would argue not so much. I have read and taught use-of-force classes using the grand jury investigation of that event. Darren Wilson's use of force resulting in the death of Michael Brown was determined to be objectively reasonable based upon the totality of the tense, uncertain, and rapidly evolving circumstances that were occurring. The United States Department of Justice investigated and initiated substantial changes in the operations of the Ferguson Police Department. The event is over for some. It will never be over for the friends and families of Michael Brown and Darren Wilson and for the many other people who became unwitting participants.

There are also lessons to be learned in the routine things police do every day that go unnoticed. To police smarter, perhaps it is not necessary for the police to engage every person for every violation they see. Perhaps it is okay for the police to disengage from a situation that no longer requires engagement. There are times when the police can walk away. There are times they can move on. They do not have to fight every fight. Cops do not like to hear this, and I do not like to say it. I was never one to back down from anything, so I get it. Also, people are testing officers every day, and it creates a slippery slope that can lead to worse problems, more physical encounters, and serious officer safety issues. This is a legitimate concern, and since each situation is different, there are no clear answers. I am not going to say Darren Wilson should not have engaged Michael Brown. Wilson made that call that day, and the history is as it is. A decision was made that Wilson was not wrong. That is just the way it worked out.

A long-since-retired chief of police in Sea Isle City, New Jersey, talked about policing smarter when he described the circumstances and death of one of his officers. Michael P. Cullinane responded to a construction accident where a man was unconscious in a belowground pit where he was working. Cullinane bravely entered the pit to save the man and was also overcome by the contaminated air that had already incapacitated the worker. Cullinane collapsed to the bottom of the pit and drowned in the water. The fire department rescued the unconscious man. The chief said that the construction worker was alive and would still be alive whether the police arrived at the scene or not. Regardless, Officer Cullinane bravely lost his life in an attempt to save another, and I am not going to second-guess his decision. Officer Michael Cullinane is a hero. We cannot change the results of his decision. History wrote that.

Many people across this country are dying because of violence. Most of these deaths are a result of random acts of violence and are not at the hands of the police. However, every death is a tragedy. Every person killed by the police, no matter how reasonable, is tragic. Every death is a wasted life. Every life lost can no longer be a son or daughter, a father or mother, a brother or sister, or a friend. Every person who dies has someone who cares about them and will experience the loss of their life.

The police cannot stop most of the violence they see. The reasons for it are multifaceted and mostly beyond the influence of the police. However, if we can do anything, we can be smarter. When possible, we should evaluate the things we are doing and find better ways to do them. We do not always have that luxury, but sometimes we do. Sometimes we can slow things down and get time on our side. It is not about not doing the job. It is not about ego. It is about being smart. Either we get smarter on our own, or the courts and our government will force it on us. We see it every day when we receive guidelines initiated from some governing agency and when we see court decisions that set forth cautions. Moreover, we see declined or remanded charges by prosecutors. All police actions are examined, recorded, and exhaustingly evaluated. All of these are telling us to be better and to be smarter.

We want every one of our cops to go home safely at night, and we want everyone we come in contact with to go home safely as well. Policing smarter can help make that happen. Smart policing can help keep our cops safe. We do not need more dead heroes. We need alive cops.

Epilogue

Some people say that policing has changed since Sir Robert Peel[78] gave us his policing theology all those years ago. They say that policing has evolved and is different than it was. While I agree that is has evolved, I do not think that it has changed all that much. There is no question that there is much that the father of modern law enforcement would not recognize, but he would not recognize much of today's world either. We do not need to go back to the nineteenth century to see the evolution.

I do not think Colonel H. Norman Schwarzkopf Sr.[79] would recognize some of the units in today's New Jersey State Police, but he would recognize his troopers. His troopers have not changed all that much since 1921, when he first became the superintendent. The mission to protect and serve the people of the state of New Jersey remains as it was. They still embrace the creed of duty, honor, and fidelity that he established. How is it then that we have this new twenty-first-century policing model that we all acknowledge is necessary? Has policing changed or not?

Policing has not changed. Technology changed, and the way we police changed. Policing remains firmly based on the United States Constitution, which has been around since 1789. It predates Sir Robert Peel, Colonel Schwarzkopf, and any other great law enforcement leaders we can name. The people defined policing. It was not the other way around.

In 1789, the people of the United States of America wrote a series of amendments to the Constitution. The fourth of those amendments explained their expectations regarding the safety and security of the people who lived in this country. The language was precise as to their expectations while remaining vague regarding its application. They knew what they wanted but were not sure how to accomplish it. Policing in American has been building on these assertations for more than two hundred years.

The Constitution, and more specifically the Fourth Amendment, has been interpreted, explained, and challenged over that time. Some of the challenges have resulted in a more detailed analysis of what the framers of the amendment considered and desired. The explanations that resulted from those challenges further define what the people expect regarding their safety and security, and the police have adapted their operations to meet the will of the people.

The most meaningful of these discussions occur among the justices of the Supreme Court of the United States. As we look back in history, cases presenting constitutional questions are rarely heard by the Court. The Court, through its discretion, carefully selects matters it will hear and ultimately renders decisions on matters that will largely impact the country. Often cases remain at lower federal or state courts, and the decisions rendered are only binding within the jurisdictions of those courts. When the Court does choose to hear a case involving a constitutional issue related to law enforcement, it is important to the police. In those instances, the Court takes notice of something and decides it will accept arguments pertaining to the safety and security of the people. Occasionally, they will hear a case involving a police action that allegedly interfered with this safety and security. Over the past fifty years or so, we have seen the Court do this in cases that implicate the Fourth, Fifth, Sixth, and Fourteenth Amendments.

Each time the Court hears arguments, it can further define, modify, or even reverse a prior decision. Sometimes these decisions result in changes to police operations, and sometimes they reinforce what departments are already doing. *Miranda v. Arizona, Terry v. Ohio, Katz v. United States, Tennessee v. Garner,* and *Graham v. Connor* are all cases that dramatically affected police operations.

Before *Miranda v. Arizona,* the police questioned people in their custody without advising them of their constitutional right to legal representation. The Court told us that pursuant to Fifth Amendment protections against self-incrimination, the police cannot do that.

Terry v. Ohio confirmed that police investigative stops of people suspected of criminal activity were not unreasonable seizures pursuant to the Fourth Amendment.

In *Katz v. United States,* the Court told us that the government cannot unreasonably infringe upon the people's right to privacy without the probable cause to do so. That case changed how the police conducted electronic surveillance and introduced the reasonable expectation to privacy doctrine.

The Court told us, in *Tennessee v. Garner,* that the states could not establish laws that circumvented the safety and security assurances of the Fourth Amendment, and the police rewrote their use-of-force policies and procedures as a result.

In *Graham v. Connor,* the Court reaffirmed and expanded on what they told us previously in *Tennessee v. Garner:* that the Fourth Amendment's reasonableness standard applies to all police uses of force because they are, in fact, seizures.

There is one common denominator in each of these cases. They all speak to the assurances granted to the people by the United States Constitution. The Constitution is the basis for all we do in policing. We do not spend time thinking about it. Most officers base their actions on department policies and procedures, but all of those policies and procedures derive from that two-hundred-year-old document. It is incredible, and I encourage you to take a moment to reflect on that. We do not do that often enough. Some never have, and some never will. If we do not take a moment to think about the history that brought us here, we miss the whole point of policing. We miss the point just like that officer who thought everything in use of force changed. He did not understand that police use of force was all about the Fourth Amendment—not about a continuum.

The same analogy applies to officers today. We need to stay within policies, but we need to do more than that. We need to understand what the policies are about, so we work in the spirit of them rather than blindly following them. Blindly following something gets people hurt and killed. We need to do more than follow. We need to function within it. For example, most police departments have a "no warning shot" policy, and police comply with it. There is nothing particularly wrong with a warning shot, and it is not constitutionally prohibited. So why do we have it? We have it because a carelessly fired round can hit an unintended target like a person.

The results of the cases I wrote about prove that policing has not changed at all. In each one of them, the Court affirmed that the Constitution and its amendments are as applicable today as they were when they were written. They represent the guarantees of the people of America that the police must vigorously guard. There is no other government representative with greater responsibility to protect those assurances.

The Constitution has not changed, and policing has not changed either. The way we police has. The police are, and will always be, the guardian of the safety and security guaranteed to people by the Constitution. The changes that do occur are procedural ones based upon rulings of the Court or are the result of technological advances we all enjoy.

Automobiles enabled the police to get to citizens quicker and led to less officer fatigue. At the same time, they created a barrier between those same citizens and the police. Communications went from light, to voice, to voice wireless, to the mobile display terminals we know today. Firearms have evolved from the single shot to revolvers to semiautomatics, and we are approaching the next generation of smart guns. Computers that did not exist are now the vehicles for one of our biggest criminal threats: cybercrime. Evidence processing has undergone remarkable advances. It was not that long ago that we were marveling at the FBI's fingerprint section. Now we solve violent personal crimes every day with DNA. The technology we use in policing has definitely changed, and they are dramatic changes that enable us to police better and smarter. However, these changes do not mean that policing, in and of itself, changed—at least not as dramatically as some of us would like to think.

Police officers still derive from the people. They are still representatives of the people just as they were two hundred years ago. When we look at the diversity in our police departments today, I believe we are moving more toward the framer's intentions of inclusiveness. Many police departments are working hard to recruit and hire officers who represent the communities they serve.

Our constitutional framers wrote down the safety and security demands of the people they represented, and for more than two hundred years, law enforcement officers have been working to guarantee that those demands are met. To this day, police officers continue to do what they have always done. You can read it on the side of many police cars: to protect and serve. To assure these constitutional guarantees, we require high standards of duty, honor, and integrity from the officers who enforce them. As we look back through law enforcement history, anytime these standards were compromised, the people rose up and demanded change. They demanded change because the Constitution guarantees that people will be safe and secure from anyone who wants to compromise it. There are no exceptions for the police. There is no police amendment to our Constitution.

I do not believe much, if anything, changed in policing, just as I do not and did not believe anything changed in use of force, as the agent suggested. I think there are times we get caught up in policing, get focused on what we are doing, and forget why we are doing it. Policing has become very complicated partly because of all of the advances we enjoy. It is hard to see how the policing of today resembles those fifty-four words of the Fourth Amendment, but if you look carefully, it is there.

It is there just like that uniform we look past to see an officer, a brother, or a sister. It is there when we look through the cop and see a person, and that is really what it is all about. It is not about the uniform, the weapons, the cars, or the technology. Policing is not about any of that. The policing I spent most of my adult life doing is so much more than that. It is what was handed down by officers who already knew what I would come to learn: that policing is about the people in their communities. Policing is about the fresh face in a community who, at some point, sees policing as a future. It is about that young man or woman who graduates from high school or college or served in the military who now applies to be a police officer. It is about the answer that an applicant gives to the question of why he wants to be a police officer. Policing is about those months in the academy, molding that future officer into what we expect from our protectors and guardians. It is the look on the face of that new officer on academy graduation day that comes from the feeling inside of him that he will rarely ever experience again. It is about that field training officer who will take that rookie and transform him into the police officer who is all things to all people. It is that officer who is now so much more than that. He is that officer who is now a part of the community. He is that officer who is a person too.

I know we are having trouble recruiting future police officers. I answered that survey the way most officers did. I do not want my family to experience what I experienced, but I am wrong about that. I am wrong because I cannot decide the future of anyone's life no matter how much I want to protect them. I am wrong because our future officers do not have to be the next victims of this job. If I believe everything I wrote in this book, and I do, then I think we are better than that. Our officers do not need to be future substances abusers or victims of suicide or die by careless or reckless behavior.

We are better than that, and we can always be even better than we are.

Do not take my word for anything you read in this book. Take some time to read the Constitution of the United States of America. If you do not want to read it, at least read the fifty-four words of the Fourth Amendment. Think about what they meant to the people who wrote them. Think about what they meant to the people they represented: the ordinary citizens. What do they mean now to you as a person, and if you are one, what do they mean to you as a police officer? What do they mean to you as a black, brown, or white police officer? Think about those words as you review your department's policies and procedures. More importantly, think about those words when you are interacting with members of your community. Think about them when you are interacting with the people you serve.

While I was writing this book, another police deadly force incident was front-page news amid all of the other things happening in our country. In June 2018, former East Pittsburgh Police Officer Michael Rosfeld shot and killed seventeen-year-old Antwon Rose II. According to the *Pittsburgh Post-Gazette*,[80] Antwon Rose II was an occupant in a vehicle suspected of participating in a drive-by shooting a few minutes earlier. Rosfeld stopped the vehicle containing three occupants, and he handcuffed one subject as two others ran from the car. Rosfeld testified that as the two ran, he thought he saw one of them raise an arm toward him, and he thought he saw a gun. According to the article, Antwon Rose II was shot by Rosfeld three times; once in the face, once in the arm, and once in the back. Rosfeld is white, and Antwon Rose was black.

Just this past week, a jury found Rosfeld not guilty of murdering Antwon Rose. I followed this trial closely, and as with other incidents I wrote about in this book, I offer no opinion. The criminal justice system decided the matter. I only know that Antwon Rose II should not be dead. However, noteworthy are comments from the Pittsburgh community as reported in the *Pittsburgh Post-Gazette*.

Questions must be urgently addressed, locally and nationally, concerning police behavior, law enforcement recruitment and police officer training ... The trial hinged upon Rosfeld's mind-set during the encounter, thirteen minutes after a drive-by shooting by another man who was in a jitney with Antwon."[81]

In a separate, but related, *Pittsburgh Post-Gazette* article, the jury foreman said,

> I felt the guy did what he had to do, but if he had to do it again, he wouldn't do it. When you're scared, adrenaline is flowing, you're on edge ... It's sad that it happened that way, but that's what happened.

Furthermore, Keith C. Burris, in a recent editorial in the same paper quoted an unnamed law enforcement expert:

> Careful recruiting and training best practices: When to shoot and when not to shoot. How to dial it down. How to follow without siren and lights until backup comes. How to deal with one suspect and one scenario at a time. How to not go from zero to 90 in seconds and to use time to your advantage. If you can get the bad guys in good time, with help, you need not be a superhero. And you may not need to shoot.

Much of what I wrote about in the chapters of this book are issues being discussed all across America, not only in Pittsburgh. All communities—black, brown, and white—are discussing police use of force. The press is reporting on police use of force and delivering editorials representing the concerns of people from all walks of life.

People are calling for the police to be better and not just in Pittsburgh. In almost every state, county, and village in this country, people are demanding more from the police. Academia, lawyers, police executives, police officers, and ordinary citizens are all asking the same question: "How can the police be better?" I believe we can be better, and I know for sure that we must be better.

We can do a better job recruiting new officers, training new officers, and continuing in-service training of veteran officers. We can do more to help our officers be more resilient to the traumas of policing and provide acceptable and safe mechanisms for officers to get help. We can adequately compensate our officers for the level of professional service we demand they provide.

It is easy to become focused and entrenched on issues to the point where we have an inability to hear and see other points of view. We see demonstrations of this every day in politics and with social issues like the environment. This is a dangerous slippery slope for all of us, but it is especially dangerous for the police who need to listen and consider the demands being made by people. The police cannot fix everything, but they should be listening and remember the guarantees set forth in our Constitution and the will of the people it was written to protect. The message is clear. The people are demanding that the police do a better job safeguarding those constitutional guarantees. We received our warning. The survival of our profession as we know it depends on what we do.

Stay safe.

Endnotes

About the Cover

1   Richard Popolow, Popolow @1986.

Chapter 1: The Fourth Amendment

2   Sir Robert Peel, 1788–1850 was a British Statesman and often referred to as the father of modern policing (Wikipedia).

3   *Roe v. Wade*, 410 U.S. 113 (1973). A landmark decision issued in 1973 by the United States Supreme Court on the issue of the constitutionality of laws that criminalized or restricted access to abortions.

4   *Miranda v. Arizona*, 384 U.S. 436 (1966). The court held that a defendant in custody makes an interrogation admissible as evidence only if law enforcement told the defendant of the right to remain silent and the right to counsel and those rights were waived

5   *Terry v. Ohio*, 392 U.S. 1 (1968). A police officer may stop a suspect on the street and frisk him or her without probable cause to arrest, if the police officer has a reasonable suspicion that the person has committed, is committing, or is about to commit a crime and has a reasonable belief that the person "may be armed and presently dangerous."

6   *Graham v. Connor*, 490 U.S. 386 (1989). All claims that law enforcement officials have used excessive force, deadly or not, in the course of an arrest, investigatory stop, or other seizure of a free citizen are properly analyzed under the Fourth Amendment's objective reasonableness standard rather than a substantive due process standard.

7   Ibid.

8   Ibid.

9   Ibid.

10 *Delaware v. Prouse*, 440 U.S. 648. Except where there is at least artic-
    ulable and reasonable suspicion that a motorist is unlicensed or that an
    automobile is not registered, or that either the vehicle or an occupant is
    otherwise subject to seizure for violation of law, stopping an automo-
    bile and detaining the driver in order to check his driver's license and
    the registration of the automobile are unreasonable under the Fourth
    Amendment.

11 *Terry v. Ohio*, 392 U.S. 1 (1968). A police officer may stop a suspect on
    the street and frisk him or her without probable cause to arrest, if the
    police officer has a reasonable suspicion that the person has committed,
    is committing, or is about to commit a crime and has a reasonable belief
    that the person "may be armed and presently dangerous."

12 *Katz v. United States*, 389 U.S. 347 (1967). It is unconstitutional under
    the Fourth Amendment to conduct a search and seizure without a war-
    rant anywhere that a person has a reasonable expectation of privacy.

13 *Scott v. Harris*, 550 U.S. 372 (2007). The Fourth Amendment does
    not prevent a police officer from ramming a fleeing suspect's car to end
    a high-speed chase, notwithstanding the risk of serious harm to the
    suspect.

14 *Tennessee v. Garner*, 471 U.S. 1 (1985). Under the Fourth Amendment of
    the US Constitution, a police officer may use deadly force to prevent the
    escape of a fleeing suspect only if the officer has a good-faith belief that
    the suspect poses a significant threat of death or serious physical injury
    to the officer or others.

15 Ibid.

16 Ibid.

Chapter 2: Prejudiced, Racist, and Biased Cops

17 Chief Lou Dekmar: "I sincerely regret and denounce the role our police
    department played in Austin's lynching, both through our action and
    our inaction, and for that I'm profoundly sorry. It should have never
    happened." LaGrange Georgia Police Department, lagrangega.org, news
    release, July 31, 2017.

18 At Kent State University on May 4, 1970, unarmed college students protesting the United States bombing of Cambodia were shot my members of the Ohio National Guard (Wikipedia).

19 The Ohio State University, copyright 2015, the Kirwan Institute for the Study of Race and Ethnicity.

20 *Gentlemen's Agreement*, Twentieth Century Fox, November 11, 1947.

21 *The Black, the Blue*, Copyright 2018 by Mathew Horace, Hachette Book Group, New York.

22 *Guess Who's Coming to Dinner*, Columbia Pictures, December 11, 1967.

23 *Tennessee v. Garner*, 471 U.S. 1 (1985). Under the Fourth Amendment of the US Constitution, a police officer may use deadly force to prevent the escape of a fleeing suspect only if the officer has a good-faith belief that the suspect poses a significant threat of death or serious physical injury to the officer or others.

24 *How Not to Get Shot*, 2018, D. L. Hughley, HarperCollins Publishers, Australia Pty. Ltd.

25 On August 9, 2014, Michael Brown Jr., an eighteen-year-old African American man, was fatally shot by a white police officer, twenty-eight-year-old Darren Wilson, in the city of Ferguson, Missouri (Wikipedia).

26 The Ohio State University Kirwan Institute for the study of race and ethnicity, "State of the Science, Implicit Bias Review, 2015."

Chapter 3: Reaction, Fear, and the Extent It Affects Us

27 CNN, January 19, 2019, Nicole Chavez, Dakin Andone, Marlena Baldacci.

28 *Highway Patrol*, 1959 Seven Network, Syndication, California.

29 *Dragnet*, 1951, Jack Webb, Los Angeles

30 *Adam-12*, 1968, NBC

31 *Left of Bang*, Black Irish Entertainment LLC, Patrick Van Horne and Jason A. Riley, 2014

32 *Violent Encounters: A Study of Felonious Assaults on Our Nation's Law Enforce Officers,* Anthony J. Pinizzotto, PhD, Edward F. Davis, MS, Charles E. Miller III, August 2006

33 Patrick Sweeney, PJsweeney.com

34 *Psychology Today*.com, Fear, Paranoia, Phobia

35 *Merriam-Webster*.com/dictionary/fear

36 *Patton*, 1970, Frank McCarthy, Twentieth Century Fox
37 Force Science Institute—through its team of physicians, psychologists, behavioral scientists, attorneys, and other leading professionals—has and continues to conduct scientific research and study of human factors as it relates to high-stress, rapidly unfolding encounters, including the intricacies of human movement, action/reaction times, how the mind works during rapidly unfolding events, and decision-making under stress. Forcescience.org, 2700 S. River Road, Suite 300 Des Plaines, IL 60018.
38 Force Science Institute Ltd., Force Science Certification
39 On April 4, 2015, North Charleston, South Carolina, Police Officer Michael Slager conducted a traffic stop of Walter Scott for a nonfunctioning brake light. That stop ended with Slager shooting Scott in the back as he was running away. Slager was convicted of second-degree murder and sentenced to twenty years imprisonment.

Chapter 4: The Cynic

40 *Rizzo's Fire*, Minotaur Books, New York, 2011.

Chapter 5: The Expendables in America

41 Energy Policy Act of 2005.

Chapter 6: The Militarization of the Police

42 The Posse Comitatus Act. Whoever, except in cases and under circumstances expressly authorized by the Constitution or Act of Congress, willfully uses any part of the army or the air force as a posse comitatus or otherwise to execute the laws shall be fined under this title or imprisoned not more than two years, or both. (Added Aug. 10, 1956, ch. 1041, § 18(a), 70A Stat. 626; amended Pub. L. 86–70, § 17(d), June 25, 1959, 73 Stat. 144; Pub. L. 103–322, title XXXIII, § 330016(1)(L), Sept. 13, 1994, 108 Stat. 2147.) Cornell Law School, Legal Information Institute
43 ArmaLite, George Sullivan Founder, 1954, Hollywood, California, Parent Organization, Strategic Armory Corps. Geneseo, IL

44 Colt's Manufacturing Company, LLC is an American firearms manufacturer, founded in 1855 by Samuel Colt. It is the successor corporation to Colt's earlier firearms-making efforts, which started in 1836 (Wikipedia).

45 Smith & Wesson is an American manufacturer of firearms, ammunition, and restraints. The corporate headquarters are in Springfield, Massachusetts. Smith & Wesson was founded in 1852, and after various corporate changes, it is now a unit of American Outdoor Brands Corporation (Wikipedia).

46 The Thompson submachine gun was invented by John T. Thompson in 1918 and became famous during the Prohibition era (Wikipedia).

47 Ibid.

48 Heckler & Koch GmbH is a German defense manufacturing company that manufactures handguns, rifles, submachine guns, and grenade launchers. The company is located in Oberndorf in the state of Baden-Württemberg, and it also has subsidiaries in the United Kingdom, France, and the United States (Wikipedia).

49 Colt's Manufacturing Company, LLC is an American firearms manufacturer, founded in 1855 by Samuel Colt. It is the successor corporation to Colt's earlier firearms-making efforts, which started in 1836 (Wikipedia).

50 The 1986 FBI Miami shootout was a gun battle that occurred on April 11, 1986, in a formerly unincorporated region of Miami-Dade County in South Florida between eight FBI agents and two serial bank robbers and murderers (Wikipedia).

51 The North Hollywood shootout was a confrontation between two heavily armed and armored bank robbers and members of the Los Angeles Police Department on February 28, 1997 (Wikipedia).

52 The Meal, Ready-to-Eat—commonly known as the MRE—is a self-contained, individual field ration in lightweight packaging bought by the US Department of Defense for its servicemembers for use in combat or other field conditions where organized food facilities are not available (Wikipedia).

53 The North Hollywood shootout was a confrontation between two heavily armed and armored bank robbers, Larry Phillips Jr. and Emil Mătăsăreanu, and members of the Los Angeles Police Department in the North Hollywood district of Los Angeles, California, on February 28, 1997 (Wikipedia).

54 The United States Navy Sea, Air, and Land Teams, commonly abbreviated as Navy SEALs, are the US Navy's primary special operations force and a component of the Naval Special Warfare Command (Wikipedia).

55 Willys was a brand name used by Willys–Overland Motors, an American automobile company best known for its design and production of military Jeeps and civilian versions during the twentieth century (Wikipedia).

56 Jeep is a brand of American automobiles that is a division of FCA US LLC, a wholly owned subsidiary of the Italian-American corporation Fiat Chrysler Automobiles (Wikipedia).

57 The Columbine High School massacre was a school shooting that occurred on April 20, 1999, at Columbine High School in Columbine, an unincorporated area of Jefferson County, Colorado, near Littleton, in the Denver metropolitan area (Wikipedia).

58 Sun Tzu was a Chinese general, military strategist, writer, and philosopher who lived in the Eastern Zhou period of ancient China. Sun Tzu is traditionally credited as the author of *The Art of War,* an influential work of military strategy that has affected Western and East Asian philosophy and military thinking (Wikipedia).

59 *Los Angeles Times*, Hugo Martin, December 28, 2018.

Chapter 7: Mental Health and Resiliency

60 Officer Down Memorial Page, Inc. Fairfax VA, Chris Cosgriff, founder.

61 Help, Educate, Lead, Prevent (HELP) Blue PO Box 539 Auburn, MA 01501.

62 Blue HELP PO Box 539 Auburn, MA 01501.

63 *Men of Honor*, 2000, Fox 2000 Pictures, Bill Badalato, Robert Teitel.

64 *On Comba*t: *The Psychology and Physiology of Deadly Conflict in War and in Peace*, 2004, PPCT Research Publications.

65 *On Killing*, 1995, Little, Brown, and Company.

66 Crisis Support Solutions, crisissupportsolutions.com.

Chapter 8: Recruitment, Hiring, and Training

67 Sir Robert Peel, 1788–1850 was a prime minister of the United Kingdom and is considered to be the father of modern policing (Wikipedia).

68 Mixed martial arts is a full-contact combat sport that allows striking and grappling, both standing and on the ground, using techniques from various combat sports and martial arts. The first documented use of the term mixed martial arts was in a review of UFC 1 by television critic Howard Rosenberg in 1993 (Wikipedia).

69 Lt. Col. David Grossman, Grossman Academy. Lt. Col. David Grossman is an internationally recognized scholar, author, soldier, and speaker who is one of the world's foremost experts in the field of human aggression and the roots of violence and violent crime.

70 *On Combat*, 2007, Dave Grossman, Warrior Science Group Inc. publishers.

71 *On Killing*, 1995, Dave Grossman, Little, Brown and Company publishers.

72 *Failsafe*, 1964, Columbia Pictures, Sidney Lumet, Max E. Youngstein.

73 *Failsafe*, 1964, Columbia Pictures, Sidney Lumet, Max E. Youngstein.

74 *On Combat*, 2007, Dave Grossman, Warrior Science Group Inc. publishers.

75 *The Guardian*, 2006, Touchstone Pictures, Armyan Bernstein, Lowell D. Blank, Zanne Devine, Beau Flynn,

76 *The Untouchables*, Paramount Pictures, Art Linson, 1987.

77 Sir Robert Peel was a British statesman who is regarded as the father of modern British policing (Wikipedia).

Epilogue

78 Herbert Norman Schwarzkopf Sr. was an American police administrator and military officer. He headed the formation of the New Jersey State Police as colonel upon its formation in 1921 (Wikipedia).

79 *Pittsburgh Post-Gazette*, March 24, 2019.

80 *Pittsburgh Post-Gazette*, March 26, 2019.

81 *Pittsburgh Post-Gazette,* March 31, 2019.

About the Author

Martin Schwartz started his law enforcement career in the United States Air Force as a security policeman. Upon being honorably discharged from the air force, he joined the Township of Franklin Police Department in New Jersey. He served in patrol, highway safety, and emergency management attaining the rank of sergeant. He spent eleven uniformed years with the police department and then joined the New Jersey Division of Criminal Justice.

While at the Division of Criminal justice, he served in the environmental crimes and insurance fraud units. He was detached to command the Domestic Violence Group of the Camden City initiative that supported the Camden Police Department. He supervised insurance fraud south before retiring in 2001.

In 2002, after a twenty-five-year career in New Jersey law enforcement, he became a special agent with the United States Environmental Protection Agency's Criminal Investigation Division (CID). His duty stations included the Federal Law Enforcement Training Center (FLETC) in Glynco, Georgia, the Philadelphia

Area Office, and the Trenton Resident Office. He was the first CID national use of force coordinator responsible for all use-of-force policy, equipment, and training. In addition, he developed and coordinated the CID's critical incident stress management and peer support unit.

After a forty-three career, Special Agent Schwartz retired from law enforcement in 2016. Currently, he is the law enforcement advisor for a major software company, Sunflower Systems.

Special Agent Schwartz (retired) is a graduate of the United States Air Force Security Police Academy, the New Jersey State Police Academy 162nd municipal police class, the Federal Criminal Investigator Training Program, the USEPA-CID National Training Academy, the Federal Law Enforcement Training Accreditation Assessor program, and the Force Science Certification course. He is a use of force, firearms, tactics, and active shooter instructor. He holds certifications in both individual and group peer support from the International Critical Incident Stress Foundation (ICISF) and the FLETC, and Suicide Prevention, Intervention, and Postintervention from the ICISF.

He has been recognized for exemplary service and bravery numerous times in his career. He is the recipient of a Medal of Honor from the New Jersey Policeman's Benevolent Association and holds awards for lifesaving with valor and meritorious service. He has numerous awards and commendations from the United States Air Force and federal, state, and local law enforcement agencies.

Schwartz is a member of the American Legion, Federal Law Enforcement Officers Association, Air Force Security Forces Association, International Association of Law Enforcement Firearms Instructors, International Law Enforcement Educators and Trainers Association, International Association of Chiefs of Police, and the National Rifle Association. He is active in critical incident stress management response and peer support training for first responders.

He may be contacted at forceanalysisconsultants@gmail.com.